LIFE AFTER DEBT

Recapitalizing the Troubled Business

LIFE AFTER DEBT

Recapitalizing the Troubled Business

EDMOND P. FREIERMUTH

DOW JONES-IRWIN
Homewood, Illinois 60430

This publication is designed to provide accurate and
authoritative information in regard to the subject matter
covered. It is sold with the understanding that the
publisher is not engaged in rendering legal, accounting, or
other professional service. If legal advice or other expert
assistance is required, the services of a competent
professional person should be sought.

*From a Declaration of Principles jointly adopted by a Committee
of the American Bar Association and a Committee of Publishers.*

Acquisitions editor: Richard A. Luecke
Project editor: Ethel Shiell
Production manager: Stephen K. Emry
Compositor: TC Systems
Typeface: 11/13 Century Schoolbook
Printer: Arcata Graphics/Kingsport

ISBN 1-55623-044-3
Library of Congress Catalog Card No. 87–72744

Printed in the United States of America

1 2 3 4 5 6 7 8 9 0 K 5 4 3 2 1 0 9 8

This book is dedicated to the numerous CEOs who have allowed me to lend a hand in a time of adversity.

PREFACE

Since 1982, I have been retained as a financial consultant by the chief executive officers (CEOs) of about 30 small- and medium-sized businesses. In most of the cases, a crisis had erupted because cash flow had come to a sudden halt. I was asked to help the CEOs overcome one or more financial, marketing, or operational problems that threatened the survival of their enterprises.

It is a regrettable fact of business life that the managers of faltering concerns unable to honor debts are held in very low regard, if not contempt, by many of their stakeholders—lenders, suppliers, and even employees. It is a widely held view that incumbent management is usually the cause of the problems and, accordingly, not capable of leading the business out of the morass.

The more a CEO's competence is questioned, the more her or his confidence is shaken. That only compounds problems, because a CEO entering the arcane world of debtor and creditor rights and insolvency law truly feels some inadequacy. Trying to comprehend the lexicon of jurisprudence while remaining responsible for the conduct of the business is an incredibly difficult assignment.

Early on I discovered a tremendous void in these individuals' understanding of the process of turning around a troubled company. I also learned that scant literature was available on the subject. So, I wrote a book—*Revitalizing Your Business*—to explain how it is done. The feedback I have received from business owners and managers as well as lenders and trade creditors has been uniformly positive.

As a matter of policy, I now require all prospective clients to read that book before we begin working together. Sometimes, but fortunately not very often, this results in my not getting an assignment that I would like to have. Some CEOs simply do not want to accept the austerity program I recommend. In the short term, this cuts down on the fees I collect for my advisory services. Over the long run, though, I have found that those CEOs who do implement the steps I suggest increase the likelihood of a successful restructuring program. I am pleased to say that most of the businessmen and businesswomen with whom I have worked are still at the helm.

During the past few years, I have learned many new techniques for recapitalizing financially troubled businesses and allowing CEOs to return more quickly to the things they do best. I sincerely believe that writing a book on the subject is the best way for me to disseminate this information to as broad an audience as possible. *Life after Debt* is the result of my effort to achieve that objective.

Life after Debt differs from the first volume I wrote on business turnarounds in one principal respect: The intended users of this book include not only harried CEOs but also attorneys, directors, insurance executives, lenders, accountants, and other outside professionals offering their services to businesses. The first book was directed specifically to the CEOs charged with managing the turnaround process in their companies.

A great many business advisers are not aware of the wide range of alternatives available to their clients who get into trouble. These professionals exert enormous influence—and deservedly so—over the decisions made by the CEOs of their clients. Although such a recommendation is made with absolutely the best of intentions, far too often the knee-jerk reaction to intense creditor pressure is the filing of a Chapter 11 bankruptcy petition.

I remain convinced that few situations require such an extreme measure. When you consider that only about 1 in 10 or 15 businesses is successfully reorganized in bankruptcy court, you have to wonder why such a course of action is pursued. I can only conclude that the decision makers did not realize other avenues were available. *Life after Debt* is intended to rectify that situation.

We will explore such topics as searching for new equity capital; pursuing a new lender; getting suppliers to accept less than the full amount owed to them; obtaining a temporary moratorium on old debts; negotiating extension programs; finding "angels"; making a general assignment for the benefit of creditors; allowing secured creditors to peacefully foreclose on collateral; selling assets at commercially reasonable prices; and many more court-administered and out-of-court options available to CEOs of financially ailing business establishments.

The opportunity to design a creative and imaginative turnaround plan is available to anyone willing to work hard to accomplish it. The purpose of *Life after Debt* is to get the reader to think of various strategies and techniques applicable to his or her problems with creditors. Think of the individual examples in this book as a type of financial menu. The ideas presented in the exhibits can be used in various combinations. It is possible, albeit unlikely, that a business might actually go through all of the various stages of difficulty depicted.

To help readers better understand why a particular recapitalization technique was used, as well as to add realism, I have made substantial use of the case method of presentation. These cases have been synthesized from actual turnarounds in which I have been involved as a financial adviser. Some of the specific programs utilized by my clients have been modified in this book to better emphasize a particularly useful strategy or technique. To preserve the anonymity of the business owners and managers of these companies, much about the scenarios depicted has been fictionalized. In addition, because the information presented has application to numerous general business situations, the first name of each entity has a common root—Generi—as in *generic.*

In writing *Life after Debt,* I have made use of a large number of off-the-record comments by CEOs, lending officers, attorneys, consultants, accountants, and others. I am very grateful for the candor of those who cooperated with me in developing this book into what I believe is a useful management tool. If the message in *Life after Debt* is received by only a small percentage of the hundreds of thousands of businesses that annually find themselves in the throes of financial difficulty, I will have accomplished the mission upon which I embarked.

Edmond P. Freiermuth

CONTENTS

INTRODUCTION

The business of America is business.

Calvin Coolidge

HOW BIG IS BUSINESS
IN THE UNITED STATES?

Free enterprise in America during the 1980s has apparently never been better. Although there are many definitions of what a business is, various publications have estimated that the number of business establishments in this country is between 5 million and 15 million. If each person who engages in a business or a profession (including sole proprietorships, partnerships, and personal service corporations) is counted as a single business unit, then the higher figure is probably closer to the truth.

And, the total is growing rapidly. A conservative measure, extrapolated from data compiled by the U.S. government, is that new business formations have averaged about 100,000 a year since the start of this decade. Broader calculations made by magazines such as *Inc., Venture, Entrepreneur,* and *D&B Reports,* which are devoted primarily to emerging business issues, place the annual figure upward to 500,000. Irrespective of who is counting, though, the size of the universe of American businesses is huge, and it is undergoing a period of dynamic growth and change.

Nearly everyone is pleased by these developments. While the country's largest commercial and industrial corporations have, in the aggregate, pared their employment rolls since the last recession, small- and medium-sized businesses have more than taken up the slack.

Despite lingering, well-chronicled problems in the smokestack industries, the farm belt, the oil patch, and their domino effect on other businesses in their geographical regions, macroeconomic statistics such as the gross national product (GNP) have been on the rise for more than five years running. The political, economic, and managerial leaders who engineered these changes are no doubt satisfied by the data. Indeed, growing our way out of our problems is high on the national agenda.

Emergence of the entrepreneurial spirit has perhaps been *the* business story of the 1980s. The opportunity to run one's own business or control one's own destiny has been acted on by literally hundreds of thousands of individuals or small groups and facilitated by legions of venture capitalists, lenders, suppliers, investment bankers, attorneys, consultants, accountants, and sundry other advisers. Many of the preceding list of professionals are, of course, themselves entrepreneurs. A very accommodating U.S. government, its agencies, and its instrumentalities have also played key roles (sometimes by playing no role at all) in the development of new business enterprises.

WEAK LINKS IN THE CHAIN

All seems well in our Camelot, but is it? Not by a long shot! There are two very severe structural weaknesses in the architectural design of the current U.S. economic expansion program. First, the service sector has come to so thoroughly dominate American economic activity that it threatens to undermine the stability of the system. Second, much of the growth achieved this decade has been fostered by the accumulation of staggering sums of debt by governmental units and the private sector.

Service Sector Now Dwarfs Rest of Economy

The U.S. Commerce Department estimates that as many as two out of every three jobs in this country are held by providers of services. The list includes not only most government workers but also employees engaged in activities relating to retail trade, utilities, wholesaling, finance, insurance, advertising, real estate, and all those kids working at the rapidly proliferating fast-food restaurants. The inexorably shrinking remaining jobs are centered in agriculture, forestry, fishing, mining, construction, and manufacturing.

Service-driven enterprises are potentially more unstable than other forms of business. The barriers to entry revolve around intellectual hurdles as much or more than physical or financial constraints. Instead of machinery and equipment bolted to the floors of manufacturing facilities, the service provider carries the means of production in his or her head. Inventories consist of thoughts and ideas as opposed to tangible goods.

The above factors have made service workers highly mobile, enabling them to pack a few boxes and move on to the next great opportunity. A large number of them have decided the time is right to set up in business for themselves. In good times, nothing could be better. In more trying periods, the inability to generate adequate cash flow will produce much angst.

Growth Financed with Borrowed Funds

Americans have a seemingly insatiable appetite for increasing their possession of material goods. The country's domestic capacity to furnish the trappings of the good life, however, is diminishing in relative terms. We have watched other industrialized nations outcompete us in the production of worldly goods.

In the short run this has had a magnificent effect on the quality of life for the average American. At some juncture, however, the industrialized nations of the world that have provided these products are going to realize that their prodigious savings and investments have allowed our citizenry to satisfy well-developed habits of conspicuous consumption. And, of course, most of our purchases have been made on credit.

In the past half-dozen years, the United States has become the world's largest debtor nation. Soon, America's international borrowings will dwarf the combined indebtedness of all its Latin American neighbors. The day may soon come when the creditor nations ask that their loans be repaid and the United States won't be able to honor the requests. Can you imagine a suggestion to the governments of Japan or West Germany that we trade some of our excess services for the automobiles they have already sent to us?

The U.S. government's deficit-spending binge was previously thought to be irresponsible, if not impossible. Only during times of war or severe recession have such huge flows of red ink been tolerated. And the fiscal actions of our leaders in Washington have set a dangerous precedent for our business owners and managers to follow.

In a very brief period of time, massive changes have been made to the consolidated balance sheet of corporate America. Enormous blocks of debt have been used to systematically reduce equity. The number and size of junk bond and lender-financed leveraged buyouts, divestitures, friendly and hostile takeovers, greenmail, and other stock repurchase transactions have been covered extensively by the media. Literally hundreds of billions of borrowed dollars have been raised for these activities. The leveraging phenomenon is not limited to the large, publicly traded companies, either. It is growing among already thinly capitalized small- and medium-sized businesses.

BUSINESS FAILURES CONTINUE RISING

Business ventures financed primarily with creditors' funds rather than equity have a great deal of upside potential, and they are undeniably exciting; they are also exceedingly risky. Consider these statistics: Dun & Bradstreet Corporation has reported that U.S. business failures—establishments closing their doors while still owing creditors—increased from 7,564 in 1979 to 61,232 in 1986. Not surprisingly, the percentage of failed service businesses has grown steadily from practically nil to more than 30 percent of the total.

For those readers with an interest in such gruesome data, the compound annual growth rate of American business mortalities has been about 35 percent over the past seven years, giving the business-of-going-out-of-business the dubious distinction of being among America's fastest-growing sectors.

As unsettling as that raw information is, the underlying problems could be much worse than they presently appear. Business failures, had they followed the usual pattern of the past six or so decades, should have steadily declined during the most recent economic expansion—among the longest since the Great Depression. One would expect fewer failures in good times. Atypically, they rose.

This does not bode well for what is likely to happen in the next economic contraction. And, unless our monetary and fiscal authorities have recently discovered the antidote for business cycles, U.S. economic history strongly suggests that businesses should be getting ready to survive another recession.

Note that the word *recession*, not depression, was used. A financial and economic debacle of the type that enveloped the world in the 1930s is not likely to recur. The elaborate system of safety nets already in place is going to prevent a collapse of the domestic and international financial markets and enable trading partners to resolve long-standing problems through negotiations.

ABLE BORROWERS WILL PAY FOR LENDERS' MISCUES

The inability of underdeveloped debtor nations to repay the principal and/or accrued interest on their loans is, and will remain, very troublesome. The large commercial banks can do virtually nothing to compel those borrowers to pay back the hundreds of billions they owe. The political and economic ramifications of implementing even more austere programs in Third World countries are so highly charged that the only realistic solution is for financial institutions to forgive a substantial portion of the debt.

The U.S. creditor banks, aided and abetted by the tacit policies of the Federal Reserve Board, have already begun to implement a program to deal with the problem of uncollectible loans to illiquid, if not insolvent, foreign borrowers. The solution is really very simple: Build up sufficient loan loss reserves from other sources and then charge off or write down the international loans that are not performing.

How can this be done? By making borrowers who *are* able to pay bear more of the burden. Only a very select few of the largest and most creditworthy borrowers can respond to higher prices on bank loans by going to other sources to obtain funds needed to run their businesses or manage their households. The rest must absorb the higher interest charges because they can neither pay off their loans nor find lower-cost alternative sources.

Using the prime rate as the base lending rate charged by banks, the real interest rate (the rate paid, less the rate of inflation) that America's best corporate borrowers have paid over the past several years has been more than double the historic norm of 3 percent to 3.5 percent. Less creditworthy business borrowers, of course, must pay premiums above the prime rate, sometimes rather steep ones. It is not as rare an event as you might think for a high-risk borrower to be required to pay prime *plus* 15 percent to obtain working capital funds.

Individuals typically pay even higher rates than most businesses do for the money they borrow on their credit cards and other installment loans. But that is the subject of another treatise. Suffice it to say, individuals are doing their part, albeit perhaps unwittingly, to help the big money-center banks solve the international debt crisis.

October 1979 Decision of the Fed

Under Chairman Paul A. Volcker's adroit stewardship, the Fed consciously and effectively managed real interest rates so as to provide creditors with real returns on their assets—provided they can collect the interest and fees they charge. This has been going on since October 1979, when the Fed changed its policies to concentrate on money supply growth rather than on interest rates. After a period of volatile changes in interest rates in the early 1980s, there has been a period of relative calm and stability.

It is more than coincidental that business failures have continued to increase steadily since 1979. This is the byproduct of the fact that the real cost of using borrowed capital has been positive during the entire period. For almost all of the 15 years preceding the Fed's change in monetary policy, it was eminently more sensible to borrow than to lend. With inflation rising faster than interest rates (many of which were fixed by Fed regulations), it literally paid to leverage-up to the maximum possible.

For the past seven or eight years, being an overextended, undercapitalized borrower has not made sense. A great many owners and managers of failed and discontinued businesses have learned that lesson firsthand. When the next recession arrives, many more casualties will be reported. That is the manner in which excesses are expunged from the system.

More Conservative Lending Environment

More than just high real interest rates work against borrowers. The regulators of financial institutions have gently, but relentlessly, tightened their grip, ever careful to avoid a crisis in confidence in the financial system as a whole. Internal auditors and outside CPAs as well have steadily sharpened their pencils and criticized loans of questionable collectibility.

Furthermore, the boards of directors and the top managers of the financial intermediaries have themselves taken increasingly tougher positions on the administration of problem loans. To the dismay of many debtors, creditors and their watchdogs have been sufficiently embarrassed by the poor overall quality of the financial system's collective loan portfolio that they now *want* to mend the errors of the past.

Although funds are, and will remain, readily available to qualified borrowers, they will continue to be both difficult and costly to obtain. In addition, to satisfy external and inside demands for improved credit quality, loan officers are more and more often requiring that marginal loans be secured.

Requests Made for Collateralized Loans

Just what constitutes a marginal loan is very difficult to ascertain. Certainly financial leverage and profitability are two of the determining factors. If a business has recently lost money and its debt-to-worth ratio exceeds 3 to 1, it is highly probable that the next time the loan is up for renewal (if not sooner) the borrower will be asked to pledge some or all of its assets to secure the repayment of the loan.

The great majority of small- and medium-sized businesses in America have little choice but to go along with such requests. They have very limited accessibility to other sources of borrowed funds—at least on more reasonable terms than they presently enjoy—and they have little or no opportunity to tap into the market for equity capital.

When managers of financially ailing concerns attempt to obtain funds from new banking sources, they are often turned down for (what appear to them) very vague reasons—"too risky," "no longer bankable," "unseasoned," "too thinly capitalized." What do such euphemisms really mean? Most lending officers don't want to, or can't afford to, spend precious time explaining what *would* make the business an attractive candidate for a bank loan. Simply too many other opportunities *do* fit their criteria.

Other lending institutions will lend money to borrowers no longer considered desirable by the banks. The asset-based financing community has become a frequently sought alternative by borrowers that no longer qualify for bank credit. Such credit arrangements are seldom, if ever, provided on bases better than those granted by banks, and they are invariably fully secured.

This is more than just a subtle change in the way the lending business is evolving. It is extremely important because having a security interest in the assets of a borrower enables the lender to exert tremendous influence over the business. The willingness of a secured creditor to work with a business that gets into financial trouble is directly related to what that lender believes is the liquidation value of the business and whether or not that amount is sufficient to repay the outstanding loan balance.

Loans to foreign borrowers are based primarily on unsecured promises. If those debtors are unable, for whatever reasons, to honor their obligations, the lenders have little choice but to negotiate. In theory, if a secured loan to a U.S. borrower is not paid in accordance with the terms and conditions on which it was made, the lender has the option to foreclose on its collateral, sell or liquidate the assets, and apply the proceeds to the loan.

Business Bankruptcies on the Rise

In practice, it is not that simple. Lenders and borrowers more often than not get into very strong disagreements about what to do in business situations where there is significant doubt as to the viability of the enterprise. An us-versus-them mentality develops on both sides. All too often the solution sought by borrowers is filing for protection under Chapter 11 of the U.S. Bankruptcy Code.

Without a doubt, that decision does give the debtor relief in the short term. If managed properly, efforts by the lender to foreclose on security interests it has been granted can be placed on hold for many months. This creates the illusion that things are better than they really are. But in the long run, the vast majority of Chapter 11 cases end up being liquidated. By some estimates, 80 to 90 percent, or more, of all businesses seeking court-administered reorganizations end up closing their doors forever. In the process, the owners of the businesses lose virtually everything they have invested, and they might also be required to suffer the ignominy of filing personal bankruptcy to get out from under their accumulated debts.

Given the appallingly low success rate of Chapter 11 turnarounds, one has to wonder why so many businesses elect to seek that solution to their problems. And yet, the number of corporate bankruptcy cases in the United States is now running at an annual rate of more than double the total filed in 1980.

Bankruptcy Court System Strained

The vast majority of the nearly three quarters of a million bankruptcy cases now filed each year involve individuals attempting to escape the clutches of the grantors of consumer loans on real and personal property as well as the issuers of credit cards. The dollar amounts of the individual cases are relatively small, but they use up a very great amount of the bankruptcy court system's time and resources.

The case overload has placed the court system itself in difficult straits. The extremely heavy workload of bankruptcy judges and the increased stress resulting from having to make decisions under less-than-ideal circumstances have jarred many of them into reevaluating whether it is worth all the trouble. Severely complicating matters is the fact that most judges earn far less as adjudicators than they could representing debtors or creditors. The demand for insolvency lawyers has become so great that an experienced bankruptcy judge can treble or quadruple his or her earnings by leaving the bench. Many are doing just that. No wonder the experience level of the current corps of bankruptcy judges is in a state of decline. No matter how bright the new judges are, they simply cannot be expected to make rulings on cases as well as their more seasoned predecessors. Something has got to be done to ease the problems of the court system designed to permit troubled businesses and their creditors to resolve problems.

Out-of-Court Solutions Growing

The most successful firms specializing in insolvency law have begun to address the problem of the overburdened bankruptcy court system by seeking out-of-court solutions to debtor/creditor problems. The limiting factor for even the best and brightest attorneys seems to be their training to think as lawyers, not as businesspeople. There are limits to the effectiveness of adversarially determined business decisions in out-of-court settings. Companies in the throes of financial difficulty frequently need to make decisions quickly, even when all the facts of the case have not been determined. Indecision may be the key to flexibility, but it can also result in the death of the business.

The National Association of Credit Management (NACM) and its nationwide affiliates have become effective alternatives to the bankruptcy court. The reason for NACM's emergence in the business turnaround arena is that its constituency is comprised primarily of tens of thousands of suppliers who have made independent decisions to extend credit to debtors on an unsecured basis. Those creditors are in desperate need of a unified voice in negotiations with the secured creditors—principally banks and asset-based lenders—who can so strongly influence the directions in which troubled borrowers are moving.

In severe cases where financially ailing businesses can't pay their bills when due, and they can no longer negotiate with unsecured general creditors on a one-on-one basis, they call on NACM affiliates to hastily convene meetings so they can explain their problems. This is the functional equivalent of inviting creditors to attend the first meeting under a Chapter 11 proceeding.

Businesses facing strong pressure from creditors can avoid using the courts and NACM affiliates altogether. For example, there is always the chance, albeit infinitesimally slim, that troubled businesses will be able to locate investors at the 11th hour. This and other topics will be discussed in greater depth in subsequent sections of this book. The possibilities are limited only by the grit, determination, and ingenuity of the individuals working on the problems. This book will, hopefully, give its readers some concrete ideas about how to search for unique applications of the general methods described herein.

> When you make a mistake, don't look back at it long. Take the reason of the thing into your mind, and then look forward. Mistakes are lessons of wisdom. The past cannot be changed. The future is yet in your power.
>
> *Hugh White*

CHAPTER 1

TAPPING INTO UNDERVALUED REAL ESTATE

The gem cannot be polished without friction, nor man perfected without trials.

Chinese proverb

Although their ranks have dwindled quickly during the 1980s, there remain a sizable number of privately owned businesses in this country that were established scores of years ago and own real estate carried on their books at very low historical costs. Creating liquidity by tapping into undervalued real estate is, without a doubt, one of the most expeditious means of recapitalizing a financially troubled business lucky enough to own such property. However, as described shortly, there are some potential pitfalls with using this strategy without first attacking the root of the difficulties.

The market for commercial and industrial real estate is one of the largest and best understood in America. Nearly every commercial bank, savings and loan association, insurance company, and pension fund in the United States has at least some part of its portfolio in real estate. Thousands of mortgage bankers and real estate brokers are knowledgeable about every facet of the local and national market for such properties. And legions of appraisers stand ready to provide an interested owner with their expert assessment of the "hidden" value of the property.

Various financing techniques exist for raising capital based on real estate assets. If a business wants, or for various reasons needs, to remain in the facilities it presently occupies, it can usually arrange to sell the property to an investor group and simultaneously lease it back from the new owners. Alternatively, the business can often borrow against its equity in the appraised market value of the property. A loan-to-value of 70 percent (less any existing liens) is quite common. Still another option is to sell the valuable property, move to a less costly location, and use the cash proceeds to finance working capital.

The temptation to use undervalued real estate as a way to solve business problems is very hard to resist, especially if the management has not previously experienced financial difficulties. The story of Generique Heating & Air Conditioning Co., Inc. (Generique), illustrates how such a decision can sometimes worsen, rather than improve, the financial condition of a business in the throes of financial setbacks.

Generique was founded in 1946 by Thomas Gentry, shortly after he returned from the war. Although it wasn't realized at the time, in a stroke of pure genius (or great luck), one of his best business decisions was to purchase property and start his company near the heart of what is now the financial center of Seattle. As its full name implies, Generique's primary line of business has evolved into designing, installing, and servicing heating and air-conditioning systems in residential and commercial structures.

Over the first 30-plus years of its existence, Generique had installed and was servicing thousands of its systems in and around Seattle. The company had become the model of what bankers seek to find in prudent and conservative management. The fledgling business was able to develop a strong relationship with one of the major banks in the city. As fate would have it, the young lending officer who granted Generique its first loan had risen to the position of executive vice president and chief credit officer in the bank. Although that highly placed bank official had long since passed the management of the Generique account to another lending officer, he and Gentry had made it a point to have a breakfast meeting at least once a year.

During its initial development, Generique utilized the credit and other services of its bank very sparingly. It borrowed only when it *had* to do so. The company always repaid its loans on time, if not in advance. Generique retained most of its earnings to finance future growth and kept its balance sheet in good condition. It maintained checking account balances in amounts that made the bank's profit on the relationship very tidy. It could be said that Generique was the ideal medium-sized business banking customer. As evidence of that fact, the company's business was solicited by nearly all of the major Seattle-area banks.

In 1978, Gentry decided the time had come for Generique to expand. Tacoma seemed the eminently logical place to start. The area had many of the same characteristics as its larger neighbor to the north, and the continued development of the airport between the two cities was sure to be of great benefit. Gentry gave the matter a lot of thought and then decided to acquire an existing company rather than start one from scratch.

Given Generique's superb track record and financial condition, its bank was more than happy to accommodate the company's request to finance the full amount of the purchase price with funds lent on an unsecured basis. The acquired company, which was to remain a wholly owned subsidiary, had achieved less impressive results than had Generique but did have the indicated cash flow to service a five-year term loan.

The all-cash transaction made the seller of the Tacoma business a relatively wealthy, and rather liquid, individual. He had agreed to continue running the business for three years while Tom Gentry's nephew gained the experience necessary to assume overall management. Unfortunately, all of that money was burning a hole in the former owner's pocket. He decided to spend a little of it on some of the finer things in life, and, with the rest, he began to speculate in a few limited partnerships investing in drilling rigs and oil and gas ventures in the Rocky Mountain states. These latter activities were a heck of a lot more interesting to him than the heating and air-conditioning business; so, he began to spend more of his time on them.

Generique's Tacoma subsidiary began to experience a deficit operating cash flow about a year and a half after the business was acquired. There were always good excuses but never any good reasons for the problems. In the early stages, the Seattle operation, which continued to produce positive cash flow, simply transferred the necessary funds to Tacoma to cover the operating shortfall. When the consulting agreement with the former owner of the Tacoma company expired, his services were terminated.

In 1981–82, Generique, like tens of thousands of other businesses, was suddenly floored by the worst recession since the 1930s. Revenues for both operations declined, while costs soared. The company began to lose money on a consolidated basis for the first time in its history. When cash flow tightened suddenly, Generique initiated a program for increasing revenues and accelerating cash receipts. Basically, the company agreed to reduce the price for its services if customers agreed to enter into prepaid contracts for annual servicing of heating and air-conditioning systems.

The program worked wonders, at least initially. Hundreds of Generique's customers signed up, and the money rolled in. The problem arose when the company had to honor those deferred service contracts. It had, in a sense, robbed Peter to pay Paul. Generique had to pay the salaries and the related expenses of employees performing the maintenance services, but it had already received, and spent, the customers' funds.

Although conceptually having customers provide what amounts to interest-free working capital is a terrific idea, this strategy only worsened Generique's problems in the long run. The company had to continually go to its bank and request a few more dollars to see it through the recession. Its loan officer at the bank was very sympathetic in the beginning, perhaps in deference to the personal relationship between the EVP and Gentry. As the losses mounted, however, Generique was "encouraged" to think about finding another bank. Only a call and a subsequent meeting with the EVP gave the company additional time to find a solution to its problems. It was made clear to Gentry that something had to be done. The EVP would not be able to intercede on Generique's behalf again.

As an interim measure, the bank agreed to provide additional short-term financing—but only if that valuable piece of property in downtown Seattle and all of the company's other assets were pledged to cross-collateralize the various loans made to Generique. Grudgingly, Gentry complied. Regrettably, the losses continued and the bank felt it could no longer support the company. The bank's account officer told Gentry that he had to find a new lender within 30 days or place the property up for sale.

In desperation, Gentry decided to sell the building. A good many people were interested in that prime piece of real estate, and the all-cash price finally paid was handsome indeed. Within the space of four months Generique was able to dispose of the property, pay off its bank loans, and move to another location. The Generique recapitalization story was a complete success, no? Not quite. The company still had not addressed its continuing problem of negative operating cash flow.

In retrospect, Generique should have directed its efforts toward controlling expenses rather than trying to increase volume in the face of increasingly strong downward pressure on prices. The problem with being so well capitalized is that it allows management to avoid confronting problems head-on for long periods of time. It really wasn't until Generique had completely broken its pick with all of its creditors and was seemingly cut off from any new external capital that it found a way to solve its problems.

Tom Gentry may have belatedly come to the conclusion that his company was in a perilous financial condition, but he did eventually institute measures to rectify matters. He sold the subsidiary purchased in 1978 back to the original owner, who had lost a great deal of money investing in energy-related activities. Gentry didn't get any cash back, but he did get a note for a few hundred thousand dollars. The former owner of the Tacoma business, with a renewed sense of interest and commitment, got busy restoring the operation to profitability.

Generique also got moving. The company dismissed 20 percent of its remaining work force of service, installation, and administrative employees. The savings in payroll, benefits, and other operating expenses were far greater than the minor loss of revenues the company experienced. The company's commission structure on installations was modified to improve profitability per job. Additionally, a new system has been established to ensure that salespersons remain involved and at risk throughout the completion of the work as well as the collection of the accounts receivable relating to installations.

Although Generique is a union shop, the events that rocked the company have imbued most of the workers with a new entrepreneurial spirit. The company has found a way to improve its billed-to-compensated-hours rate to something over 80 percent, up from just below 70 percent. This means that operating efficiency has improved to the point that the business is again cash flow positive.

Another decision Gentry made some time ago was to institute a cost-reduction plan concerning employees who use service vehicles for transportation to and from their work centers. Each affected employee is being charged for such personal use if it is beyond a five-mile radius. A number of service vehicles no longer needed in the business have been sold. The cash proceeds from the sales have been nominal, but significant insurance, maintenance, and operating expenses have been eliminated. Other expenses are under constant scrutiny, and additional savings will be produced.

Generique has gotten back to its roots. The company has returned to profitability and reestablished itself as a viable competitor in its marketplace. There is every reason to believe that Generique, with careful attention to detail, can regain its high profile in the communities it serves. Despite the company's financial ailments, it was able to provide good service to its customer base.

As noted at the outset of this chapter, it is one thing for a business to be able to unlock the equity in undervalued real estate assets it owns; it is an entirely different matter to think you can use such a recapitalization technique to solve financial problems that threaten the health of the enterprise. In the next chapter, we explore the case of a business that does not have any real estate assets to bail it out of its troubles.

CHAPTER 2

OBTAINING THAT ELUSIVE EQUITY CAPITAL

The miracle, or the power, that elevates the few is to be found in their industry, application, and perseverance under the promptings of a brave, determined spirit.

Mark Twain

Right at the outset of this chapter, it is important to state that the author's professional experiences have shown this recapitalization strategy to have a great deal of risk and an inordinately low probability of success. Having led off with that caveat, however, it must also be said that for those few who do succeed in finding a new source of equity capital at a time when it is absolutely needed, the rewards can be very, very substantial. That, no doubt, accounts for the decision of most entrepreneurially driven owners and managers of financially ailing businesses to give this idea serious thought before pursuing other avenues.

The following case should give the reader an idea of what it takes to accomplish the objective of finding an investor when the chips are down. Generik Precision Engineering Company, Inc. (Generik), is a Boston-area–based manufacturer of precision-molded interconnecting devices used by a growing number of makers of data processing, business communications, and industrial automation equipment.

The company was founded in 1976 by Gene Smithson, chairman and CEO, and Erik Cummens, president. They thought the name of the company was rather clever since it fused their first names. Both men have engineering backgrounds and had previously worked for one of the major technology companies in Massachusetts. Smithson also earned an M.B.A. from a well-known, eastern business school.

This is how Generik got into trouble. From its inception, the company began developing proprietary interconnect devices. In the formative years, the emphasis was on *quality*. The manufacturing employees, the sales force, and the rest of the staff performed very well as a team. An excellent relationship was established with one of the big banks in Boston, and the company prospered.

Then came the computer game and personal computer phenomena. It didn't take the movers and shakers in the PC market very long to discover that Generik was a great company with which to do business. Generik's management realized that with just a few minor modifications, the company could produce lower-cost, lower-quality, higher-volume products to connect microprocessors, keyboards, monitors, and printers.

Revenues were soon exploding at Generik. To handle the demand for its products, the company leased a new 100,000-square-foot facility and then moved all of its operations to that location. To keep up with rapidly expanding working capital requirements, Smithson and Cummens repeatedly asked their bank to increase the size of their company's credit facilities. The bank honored the requests of this profitable customer; but, as Generik's debt-to-worth ratio began to climb, the bank required the owners to provide additional support for the loans. First, it was their personal guarantees. Then it was a second mortgage on their residences.

Everything was fine until the shakeout occurred in the PC market. The financial difficulties surfaced quickly. Inventories became bloated as the good customers canceled orders and the not-so-good customers refused shipments. Uncollectible accounts receivable soared. Just about anything that could go wrong, did. When the accountants finished their audit and the dust cleared, Generik's income statement and balance sheet were devastated.

Long before Generik's outside CPAs completed the financial statements, Smithson and Cummens, the company's banker, and others realized that a problem of major proportions was in the making. Two months before Generik's fiscal year-end the company's management had sat down with bank officers to discuss the situation. Generik was not yet in default under any of the terms and conditions of its loan agreements, so the bank could do little more than offer advice in the strongest possible language that the company should immediately seek to find a new source of equity to help it get through the tough period that loomed ahead.

At the loan officer's suggestion, Gene Smithson made contact with an investment officer in the venture capital subsidiary of the bank's parent company. He was taken aback slightly by the person at the other end of the line, who asked that Smithson send her a copy of the company's investment memorandum, or business plan, before they got together. Gene certainly knew what a business plan was, but despite the fact that he was the CEO of a fast-growing multimillion-dollar business, he had never done one before. When he explained that he didn't have one to send, the venture capitalist said that they would not be able to meet until one was ready.

Feigning igorance, Smithson asked the investment officer if she would be kind enough to send him a letter explaining what the various parts of such a document were. Not wishing to offend the bank officer who had referred Generik to her, she agreed to send an outline of the things that should go into a plan. That information is presented in Exhibit 2–1. (The willingness of a venture capital company to offer advice on this subject is not typical. Investment officers receive so many well-prepared proposals that they don't want to waste time telling would-be prospects how to write an investment memorandum. In reality, such a request would probably be interpreted as an indication that the person asking for the information is not a very savvy manager. Were it not for the bank's connection, Smithson would have been politely rebuffed.)

As soon as Smithson received the letter from the venture capitalist, he went down to Erik Cummens' office to discuss it. Both men were struck with how detailed the investment memorandum apparently needed to be. They wondered if it wasn't just the conservative nature of the bank-related venture firm. So they decided to discuss the subject with a few of Smithson's B-school friends who had gone into the field. Much to their

EXHIBIT 2–1

Letter Outlining the Contents of an Investment Memorandum

Mr. Gene Smithson
Chairman and CEO
Generik Precision Engineering Company, Inc.
Route 128, Box 1234
Peabody, Massachusetts 01960

Dear Mr. Smithson:

Thank you very much for your inquiry. We are most appreciative of the opportunity to discuss alternative strategies which might enable Generik to finance its growth in the most profitable and productive manner. From your brief description over the phone, it seems that your company is on the threshold of becoming substantially larger in its field. That is certainly one of the things that is of keen interest to us.

As we discussed, a comprehensive investment memorandum should be prepared as soon as practicable. The final product should enable any sophisticated reader to very quickly assess the strengths, weaknesses, opportunities, and threats impacting upon Generik and, accordingly, make a quick, well-reasoned decision as to whether or not the company represents an attractive investment.

Generally speaking, an investment memorandum should be comprised of the following parts:

I. *Introduction.*
This section summarizes the proposal and includes data such as the amount and intended use of the capital; terms of the financing (including type of security, dividend or interest rate, and conversion features); five years of historical revenues and pretax income; a current, condensed balance sheet showing actual and pro forma data; a brief description of Generik's current and future business potential; and a synopsis of the primary merits of financing the company.
II. *Detailed Historical Financial Data.*
A. Five years of income statements.
B. Three years of balance sheets.
C. Three years of sources and uses of funds.
III. *Detailed Financial Projections.*
A. Cash flow forecast for next 12 months.
B. Three years of income statements.
C. Three years of balance sheets.
D. The assumptions used in preparing the data.
E. This is the most crucial aspect of the memo and should include several different scenarios (e.g., a worst-case analysis, an optimistic outlook, and a most probable scenario).
IV. *Detailed Description of the Business and History of Generik, in Narrative Form.*
A. Nature of the business—historical, current, and future (especially, the proprietary products relating to precision interconnecting devices).

EXHIBIT 2–1 (*continued*)

    B. Nature of the market.
       1. Define end-user market size.
       2. Is the need for Generik's products already recognized or must prospective customers be educated?
       3. Can the need for the products be filled in other ways? Are there substitution products or materials?
       4. How does the competition satisfy the needs of the market?
       5. How big is the market, and how fast is it growing?
       6. Who are the primary competitors, and how large a market share do they have?
       7. How severe is price competition in the market, and is it possible to insulate the company from these effects?
       8. Is Generik dependent upon a few major customers or does it have a broad base?
       9. Is the market particularly sensitive to cyclical changes in the economy?
    C. Analysis of products.
       1. Are the proprietary products protected by patents?
       2. Are there rapid changes occurring in the state of the art? Is obsolescence a factor?
       3. Product direct costs at present; effect of large increases/decreases in volume?
       4. Are there any potential servicing problems once the products are delivered to customers?
       5. Are there any significant warranty problems?
    D. Employee composition.
       1. Number engaged in highly skilled positions.
       2. Number employed in routine manufacturing.
       3. Number involved in research and development.
  V. *Summary of Current Year Operations.*
  VI. *Management, Owners, and Directors.*
     A brief biography on each of the principal members of management should be included in this section. Also provide a listing of the major shareholders; financial transactions between the company and owners/managers; and a schedule of the remuneration of the principal officers of Generik for the past two years.
  VII. *Miscellaneous Information.*
     Past, pending, and threatened legal actions, both as defendent and plaintiff; status of taxes; industry studies; names of accountants, attorneys, bankers, etc.

    I realize that developing the above outline into a full-blown investment memorandum is a formidable task. However, most of the information is probably readily available, and your accounting department can do much of the remaining numbers crunching.
    I believe that going through such an exercise will be quite valuable to you, irrespective of the outcome of your search for capital. It will, hopefully, strengthen your position about the prospects of Generik's proprietary products; it might also lead you to conclude that, although conceptually sound,

EXHIBIT 2–1 *(concluded)*

the economics, risks, and potential financial returns are inadequate. In either case, you will have developed better information upon which to make your decision.

As I mentioned over the phone, I would be pleased to make myself available on a periodic basis to offer constructive criticism to the development of the investment proposal. Again, Mr. Smithson, thank you for giving our firm the opportunity to be of service and to evaluate the potential of making an investment in Generik.

Very truly yours,

President
Bank Holding Company
Venture Capital Subsidiary

chagrin, the message was repeated over and over again—if you want to have any chance of getting money from sophisticated investors, you must lay out a compellingly good story.

Despite these admonitions from knowledgeable professionals, neither Smithson nor Cummens were especially enthused at the prospect of having to spend a lot of time and effort in preparing such a lengthy document. It wasn't that they were afraid of hard work, simply that there wasn't enough time in the day to solve the growing problems of Generik *and* try their hands at, what seemed to them to be, creative writing. The thought crossed their minds that perhaps an investment banking firm would be able to help them. Smithson also had several friends who had decided to go into the business of raising capital for companies.

Once again they were disappointed by what they heard. The "name" investment bankers were not interested in small deals like Generik under good conditions; in a time of possible crisis, there was no way for them to help. A few possibilities did surface. However, those investment bankers who did express an interest in assisting Generik's management in preparing a comprehensive selling document wanted prepaid, *nonrefundable* fees of about $20,000.

Under the circumstances, such a fee arrangement is entirely justified. Most financial pros realize that the chances for raising funds while operating under great pressures are very slim. No one is interested in working for free, which would be the probable result if an investment banker agreed to accept an engagement with Generik on a contingency basis.

After much soul searching and debate, they decided that if Generik were going to succeed, they were going to have to make a superhuman effort. They agreed between themselves that Smithson would be the point man on the investment memo and Cummens would assume even more of the responsibilities for Generik's day-to-day operations.

They then met with their bankers to explain their plans. They were surprised at the response they received. The bankers thought the idea had such a small chance of succeeding that it did not warrant the effort. They would rather see all of the managerial talent in Generik focused on a business turnaround—forget about the pipe dreams of raising new equity and get on with the program to get the bank's loans repaid.

Once again, Smithson and Cummens huddled, and they decided to "bet the company" (and most of their personal assets, since they had individually guaranteed and secured the loans from the bank). They would go along as planned. As noted earlier, this strategy is very dangerous and has a low probability of achievement. It is one of the true tests of one's mettle.

During the ensuing two months, Generik's management developed a new strategic plan wrapped around the proprietary products that had made the company successful before the PC revolution. All the while, Smithson devoted virtually all of his free time—including weekends and evenings—to writing the investment memorandum that everyone had said was so crucial to the company's success. It was a very good document.

They were very pleased with the result, and Generik's account officer at the bank also thought the company was on the verge of a breakthrough. He did not, unfortunately, have a whole lot of support from his superiors. Still skeptical of Generik's prospects, they were increasing the pressure on him to get tougher with management. It is not easy for a loan officer to remain supportive of a borrower when the credit folks start to bear down. Generik was exceedingly fortunate to have a person as strong as the loan officer was. Otherwise, it would have been all but impossible to accomplish what they ultimately did.

With the well-written business plan in hand, Smithson began his search for the heretofore elusive equity capital. By preparing the document himself, Smithson was intimately familiar with its every aspect. Consequently, he was able to make very persuasive presentations to all of the venture capitalists he was able to meet.

Despite the accolades Smithson received for his impressive turnaround plan for Generik, the bottom line was, everyone was frightened out of their wits about what was going on in the PC market. The venture capitalists could not (or perhaps more accurately, would not) make the giant leap forward as management had done in concluding that Generik's salvation rested on its proprietary products. After getting rejects from a dozen venture firms, Smithson concluded that that avenue was simply not going to lead Generik out of its continuing problems. He and Cummens became despondent for a few days and began to think their critics were perhaps correct.

Indomitable spirits that they are, Generik's owners took some deep breaths and went back to the search. They broadened their network of prospective investors to include some of Generik's customers, suppliers, and competitors. They sent copies of the business plan to about 30 of those organizations. Nearly every one sent their condolences—along with their decision to decline the opportunity to invest in Generik.

One of Generik's customers, a corporation listed on one of America's principal stock exchanges, saw something it liked. The top engineering and marketing people were dispatched to visit with Generik's owners. They reported back to their senior managers that Generik did indeed have some very good things going for it. In particular they liked the high-quality interconnecting devices Generik manufactured. Negotiations began in earnest. After more than three weeks of intensive investigation, the large public company was ready to meet with Generik's owners.

Smithson and Cummens were not prepared for the offer they received. The larger company was not interested in *invest-*

ing in Generik; it wanted to *buy* all of the company. Each of the owners would receive $1 million in cash for their stock and would receive management contracts for three years to continue in the same capacity in which they were then serving. Smithson and Cummens were at once disappointed and elated. They both felt that if Generik were given more time the problems could be solved. Down the road, the company would be worth much more than the value placed on the stock now. On the other hand, the pressure from the bank was growing more intense by the day. In addition, Generik was beginning to have trouble staying current with its suppliers.

The time had come for Generik's owners to decide. They concluded that it would be better for Generik to become a subsidiary of a public company with deep pockets than for them to continue swimming against the stream and risk it all. Although it took several weeks to effectuate closing the transaction, Generik's relationships with its bankers and its suppliers improved dramatically. The loan officer's support proved invaluable for Smithson and Cummens. The author is of the opinion that their decision was an eminently good one. They don't know how close they came to losing everything.

In the next chapter we will see what happens when the management of a business loses the support of its banker and is asked to find a new home.

CHAPTER 3

RESTRUCTURING OR REFINANCING BANK DEBT WHEN THE PRESSURES ARE BUILDING

Knowledge comes, but wisdom lingers. It may not be difficult to store up in the mind a vast quantity of facts within a comparatively short time, but the ability to form judgments requires the severe discipline of hard work and the tempering heat of experience and maturity.

Calvin Coolidge

There was a time when a great debate in credit training for commercial bank lending officers revolved around the question "Should the loan officer who makes (or who subsequently manages) a loan that goes sour be responsible for collecting it or should a credit officer specially trained for the job be assigned the task?" Among the larger banks in the country, at least, there no longer seems to be much of a debate. At the first sign of trouble, the specialists are brought into the account relationship. Bankers, like the business men and women they finance, are discovering that the sooner a problem is recognized and addressed, the higher the probability of finding a workable solution. For lenders that means full recovery of the principal and interest on loans.

The two primary early warning signs for bankers are operating losses and too much leverage. The first category obviously indicates a business experiencing problems. Commercial loan officers used to delve into the reasons for a company's troubles and search diligently along with the business's managers to find a solution. Nowadays, the trigger is pulled much more quickly. Rather than work to rehabilitate the business, banks now prefer to err on the side of conservatism, even if it means losing a formerly creditworthy customer. It is more cost effective to solve the problem by getting rid of it quickly than to try working it out.

The factor that has most enabled this shift in bank credit policy is the growth, over the past 20 years, in the number and size of asset-based lenders. These organizations are built on the assumption that risk can be profitably managed if adequate procedures and controls are installed *and* constantly monitored. The added cost of performing these functions must also be compensated. Virtually every major bank or bank holding company has purchased or formed one of these alternative sources of business finance. The business development officers of these hard-asset lending institutions are constantly searching for companies that may have "stubbed their toe" but can still qualify for secured loans.

The second red flag, excessive leverage, may or may not result from poor operating performance; but it is nevertheless one of the principal reasons borrowers are being asked to take their business elsewhere or to change the structure of loan arrangements—that is, collateralize the credit. How much debt will cause a banker to begin to feel uncomfortable? It all depends on the type of industry, of course, but well-established standards for banking industry executives to follow have been compiled for more than six decades by Robert Morris Associates (RMA), a Philadelphia-based trade group.

The financial ratios that appear in RMA's Annual Statement Studies are used extensively by loan and credit officers in determining the ongoing creditworthiness of their banks' customers. Financial data on scores of businesses in hundreds of industries (segregated into Standard Industrial Classification codes) are analyzed every year. The ratios computed are then arrayed. The median is the ratio value that falls midway between the strongest and the weakest ratios. The figure that lies between the median and the strongest value is the upper quartile. And the figure between the weakest ratio and the median is the lower quartile.

Suffice it to say, if a business's debt/worth ratio is in the upper quartile (usually less than 1.0/1.0), it will be a highly desired customer of the bank and will more than likely be able to borrow on an unsecured basis and repay the loan strictly from internally generated cash flow. If the leverage ratio lies near the median (in the range of 1.0/1.0 to 2.0/1.0), the borrower will enjoy the privilege of being able to obtain funds from its bank primarily on its ability to generate cash flow from profits to repay the debt. However, as the company edges closer to the 2.0/1.0 figure, it may need to offer collateral, such as a security interest in accounts receivable, as an abundance of caution. Probably only a periodic update will be required as to the status of the collateral. This is sometimes called a "desk drawer" secured loan because active monitoring is not deemed necessary.

If the debt/worth ratio falls near the lower quartile (in the range of 3.0/1.0 to 4.0/1.0), let the borrower beware. The ice gets pretty thin out there, and one errant step could get the business in deep trouble. This degree of leverage will almost invariably require the borrower to secure the bank's credit facility with all of the assets of the business and probably mean the owners of the enterprise must personally guarantee the repayment of the loan as well. Close monitoring of the collateral will be the order of the day, and frequent visits by loan officers will be necessary. As long as the business remains profitable, the bank will continue to provide growth financing.

The combination of operating losses and a debt/worth ratio exceeding 3.0/1.0 sets off a loud alarm for bankers. No amount of rationalizing, nor connections with senior bank officers, will succeed in keeping such a borrower in the bank. This doesn't necessarily mean the business can no longer be financed; it just means the business must find another type of lender to provide the funds. The case of Generipak Flour Mills, Inc. (Generipak), illustrates how quickly a relationship can deteriorate and the lengths a business may be required to go to retain access to external sources of funding.

Generipak was founded in the Midwest's vast grainbelt in 1925 by Werner Monck. As the name of the business implies, the company is engaged in milling various kinds of grain into a variety of flour products. A short digression is needed here to provide a little background information. Monck was a very conservative German businessman who sold his company and moved with his family from his native country in 1922. He had become very wary of the economic conditions that existed in Germany. He didn't know then how right his instincts were, but he would soon find out.

In 1923, while trying to decide how to reinvest his funds in a new American business venture, he watched what was happening in his homeland in disbelief. As recorded in H. G. Wells' *The Outline of History*, during January 1923 the value of one U.S. dollar rose from five gold marks to over 7,000. In February, the gold standard in Germany was abandoned, and the dollar to paper mark appreciated to more than 21,000. By year-end, the dollar reached the astounding value of 4 *billion* paper marks. What followed was one of the bleakest periods of German economic history. The virulent inflation literally gave way to a barter economy as paper money ceased to have any meaningful value. The economy collapsed.

Monck was deeply influenced by those events for the remainder of his long life. He was elated to have escaped the nightmare with his dollar-denominated investment. Had his timing been off by just a few months he could have been financially destroyed. Monck decided the business he was to invest in would need to be driven by staples. What could be more basic than milling flour? Irrespective of changing economic conditions, people would always need to eat. That is the basis on which he established Generipak. Through contacts reestablished with other émigrés from his province in Germany, he determined that a need existed for a mill in central Iowa.

Over the next five years, Generipak grew into a prosperous little operation. Monck and his family lived relatively ascetic lives as he retained virtually all of the company's profits to finance the business. The Great Depression of the 1930s ruined many overextended businesses; but, because Monck had an aversion to borrowing money, Generipak was not among the casualties. Indeed, as competitors fell by the wayside, Monck acquired their assets at liquidation prices. He was confident that the economy would eventually rebound.

For more than 50 years, Monck operated his business very conservatively and very profitably. His son, Hans, had joined in managing various aspects of the company, but Werner Monck

clearly made all of the key decisions, particularly those involving matters of finance. For years, Generipak's business was solicited by local lending institutions. Monck, however, was reso-
lute in not wanting any financial advice *or* money. This
antediluvian attitude, in the opinion of many inside and external observers, was responsible for stunting Generipak's growth.
Financing operations almost entirely through retained earnings
severely limited the company's opportunities.

Despite Monck's penchant for keeping Generipak's financial affairs a private matter, by the mid-1970s it became known
that the company's annual revenues had reached more than $25
million and pretax profits were slightly in excess of $1 million.
Generipak was the quintessential prospect for commercial loan
officers in search of middle-market borrowers—a long history of
profitable operations, a very low debt/worth ratio, and excellent
prospects for future growth. The only obstacle, of course, was
Werner Monck. And since he still owned all of Generipak's
stock, the status quo would probably be maintained.

Only the passage of time would change the manner in
which Generipak would be managed. As it must happen for all
of us, the elder Monck was forced by old age and failing health to
give up the reins. In 1976, at the age of 87, Werner Monck
finally retired from active management. His son was installed
as chairman. The "younger" Monck, though, was then 62 and
thinking about retiring. He had earned a very decent living and
had acquired a comfortable nest egg as his father's key lieuten-
ant. His outside interests were broader than the flour business,
and he wanted to spend more time pursuing them.

His wishes were more than easily satisfied because the next
person in line in the family-run business was Herman Folker,
aged 43, the only son of Werner Monck's daughter. With Hans
Monck's blessing, he was appointed president of Generipak as
well as its de facto CEO. In 1977, Werner Monck passed away.
His wife had died 10 years before. The ownership of Generipak
rested in the hands of Hans Monck and Herman Folker, who had
inherited his deceased mother's stock. Each of the officers held a
50 percent interest in Generipak.

Folker was, in many respects, the antithesis of his grandfather. He was aggressive and more than willing to take risks. He
had urged, unsuccessfully, that Generipak be run with more

advanced financial management techniques (that is, he wanted to prudently leverage the business). Folker had a strong formal education, and he made contacts with other entrepreneurial spirits. He received his bachelor's degree at one of the top universities in Iowa. He then earned his M.B.A. at one of the prestigious Ivy League schools. Folker could have worked in any number of other business settings, but he had thought he would be given an early chance to run Generipak. The time stretched out to 15 years. He was champing at the bit when the opportunity finally arrived.

At about the time Herman Folker assumed operating control of Generipak, many of the U.S. money-center banks were setting in motion grand designs to build their domestic lending business primarily by actively seeking new relationships with middle-market companies—those with annual sales of between $20 million and $250 million. Quite logically, given its geographic location and its already-extensive involvement in this type of lending, one of the major banks in Chicago targeted agribusiness as one of its principal areas of growth. The bank actively stepped up its recruiting of bright, ambitious M.B.A.s who were capable of quickly assessing the business plans of prospective borrowers and converting those ideas into creative, perhaps even imaginative, loan proposals.

It didn't take long for an aggressive lending officer from this bank and Folker to find each other. (The network of business school contacts reaches deep into the privately owned business community.) You can probably imagine what happened next, so it won't be necessary to tell you all the details. In a nutshell, Generipak borrowed $5 million on an unsecured basis to substantially expand its operations. Even with this large increase in bank debt and growth in accounts payable of another $2 million, Generipak still had a debt/worth ratio of just over 1.4/1.0, well within the range of a prudent banker's comfort zone.

Within two years, the company nearly doubled plant capacity, increased its customer base through an active marketing program, and developed a strategic plan to become a vertically integrated agribusiness. You may recall that during the mid-1970s, a rapid expansion of the U.S. economy's agricultural sector was generally perceived as an important counterbalance to the country's dependence on foreign oil.

Generipak's business boomed. By 1980, annual sales had increased to over $60 million. Although the company's profit margin had declined to less than half of its preexpansion level, it was generally perceived that the drop was temporary—the price that needed to be paid to enter new markets and introduce new products. And, after all, Generipak was continuing to earn almost $1 million a year before taxes. At the time, the relationship with the bank and other creditors could not have been much better. Periodic visits to Chicago, which Folker and his wife thoroughly enjoyed, included meetings with senior bank officials, who expressed their appreciation for being able to finance Generipak.

The mutuality of respect and good feelings disintegrated with the onset of the recession of 1981–82. Generipak, like many other businesses resting on a weakening base of commodity-driven products, found itself with too much capacity. Despite all-out efforts to keep volume up, including acceptance of previously avoided potential customers who had unsatisfactory credit histories, sales declined by more than 5 percent in 1982. Worse yet, Generipak *lost* $1.3 million. This was the first time anyone could ever remember that happening.

Tight cash flow was something with which Generipak's management had never had to deal. The company had always paid its bills promptly, but it now discovered it could no longer do so. Folker requested a meeting with his account officer to arrange for additional financing. Over the next week, the bank's credit department carefully scrutinized Generipak's financial statements. A rather serious deterioration had occurred in the company's financial condition. The operating loss for the prior year had caused Generipak's debt/worth ratio to increase to 2.5/ 1.0. When Generipak's account officer arrived at the company's headquarters, he was accompanied by a gentleman whose business card carried the following title: Senior Vice President and Manager—Special Assets Department.

Folker had never heard of such a bank officer before, but he quickly found out what the SVP's job was. The bank wanted to help as much as possible, Folker was informed. However, the credit arrangement would need to be changed from an unsecured to a secured status. When asked how much more money Generipak needed to get through this period of financial difficulty, Folker responded that $500,000 should be sufficient. (By advancing additional funds, the bank would satisfy a requirement that adequate consideration be provided for its receipt of a security interest in the assets of Generipak.) The SVP stated that the bank was prepared to provide this additional financing, if Generipak would agree to secure the bank's loan. The proposal initially seemed reasonable to Folker, but that was before he received the letter shown in Exhibit 3–1.

EXHIBIT 3–1
Commitment Letter Outlining Proposed New Credit Arrangement

Dear Mr. Folker:

Subject to the general terms and conditions described in this letter, which remain to be formally documented in a manner acceptable to our legal counsel, we are pleased to advise you that our bank is prepared to make available to Generipak Flour Mills, Inc., the following credit facility:

A secured, revolving line of credit equal to the *lesser* of $5,500,000 or the Borrowing Base as defined below.

The above described credit accommodation shall be governed by a Credit and Security Agreement, which shall include the following terms and conditions.

I. *Interest Rate.*
Prime plus 2½ percent, floating, payable monthly.

II. *Purposes.*
Repayment of existing unsecured bank indebtedness as well as financing for future working capital requirements.

III. *Expiration Date.*
The commitment will be reviewed at least annually at the end of the fourth month following the close of Generipak's fiscal year-end. If the company is in conformance with the terms and conditions of the Credit and Security Agreement, the commitment shall be renewed. If Generipak is not in conformance, the bank may elect to call the loan and exercise its rights as a secured creditor.

IV. *Borrowing Base.*
At no time shall Generipak's indebtedness to this bank exceed the following limits—
A. 80 percent of eligible accounts receivable;
B. PLUS 35 percent of qualified inventory, up to a maximum loan on this collateral of $1.5 million;
C. PLUS 60 percent of the "liquidation value"—less any existing encumbrances—of machinery, equipment, and real estate, up to a maximum loan on this collateral of $750,000.

EXHIBIT 3–1 (continued)

V. *Security Interests.*
Generipak will assign all now-owned and hereafter acquired accounts receivable, inventory, machinery, equipment, leasehold improvements, leasehold interests, and proceeds from any of those properties, as collateral for the loans. All appraisals, collateral exams, lien searches, and UCC filings must be completed prior to the loan closing with results approved by the bank's legal counsel.

VI. *Guarantees.*
Both of Generipak's shareholders and their spouses must execute personal guarantees of the company's indebtedness to the bank. The guarantees will be secured by second mortgages on the residences of the owners. Signed personal financial statements of the guarantors must be submitted prior to the loan closing.

VII. *Subordination Agreements.*
Any and all amounts now owing to the shareholders of Generipak, will be subordinated to the loans of the bank.

VIII. *Documentation Fee.*
Generipak will pay for all of the reasonable expenses incurred by the bank in connection with the preparation, execution, and delivery of the Credit and Security Agreement and other documents relating to the transaction; however, the maximum expense reimbursement shall be limited to $25,000.

IX. *Affirmative Covenants.*
Generipak will—
  A. Submit monthly accounts receivable aging within 15 days of the end of the previous month.
  B. Provide monthly inventory reports within 15 days of the end of the previous month.
  C. Submit updated appraisals of machinery, equipment, and real property within two months of the end of Generipak's fiscal year-end.
  D. Provide quarterly, company-prepared, financial statements within 45 days of the end of the preceding three months.
  E. Provide annual, CPA-audited, financial statements within four months after the end of Generipak's fiscal year-end.
  F. Submit a quarterly certificate signed by the CEO or CFO of Generipak stating that the company is in compliance with all of the terms and conditions of the Credit and Security Agreement.
  G. Permit the bank to conduct collateral examinations as deemed necessary by the bank; however, such reviews shall occur at least twice each fiscal year.
  H. Maintain adequate insurance coverage; CFO to furnish an annual certificate stating that Generipak is in compliance with this provision.
  I. Designate the bank as the loss-payee on all insurance proceeds.

EXHIBIT 3–1 (concluded)

   J. Maintain a ratio of current assets to current liabilities of no less than 1.15 to 1.

   K. Limit month-end finished goods inventories to 16⅔ percent of annualized sales.

   L. Maintain a ratio of total debt to tangible net worth of less than 3.0 to 1.

   X. *Negative Covenants.*
      Generipak will *not*—
      A. Encumber or permit liens other than those which are presently existing or which are part of this proposed transaction.
      B. Incur any other indebtedness unless approved by the bank.
      C. Dispose of any property except in the ordinary course of business.
      D. Enter into any new leasing agreements unless approved by the bank.
      E. Make additions to plant and equipment in excess of the preceding fiscal year's net income plus noncash charges such as depreciation.
      F. Declare or pay any cash dividends if such payment should cause Generipak to be in violation of any covenant.
      G. Repurchase or retire any common stock if such action should cause the company to be in violation of any covenant.

The above outline is purposely comprehensive. We believe that your agreement on these general terms and conditions will expedite the documentation process and facilitate an early loan closing. If you are in agreement, please sign and return this letter of understanding at your earliest convenience. Unless extended by this bank, in writing, this commitment will expire 31 calendar days from the date of this letter.

We are greatly appreciative of the opportunity to be of service to your company, and we hope that you will accept our offer to provide this financing arrangement.

Yours truly,

Jon D. Matthews
Vice President

Agreed and Accepted:

Generipak Flour Mills, Inc.

By: _____
    Herman M. Folker
    President and CEO

Date: _____

When Folker received this letter, he became quite upset. He immediately called to complain. The bank officer suggested it might be a good idea to meet again—this time in Chicago. The meeting was held in one of the sparsely furnished conference rooms of the special assets department. After Folker had a chance to express his displeasure, the SVP said that although the new credit arrangement was priced much higher (the interest rate on the current loan was prime plus one-half percent) and more restrictive than the current one, the bank would have to insist on its terms and conditions. Folker was thereupon invited to find alternative financing arrangements.

He left that meeting in a furious rage, determined to find a more cooperative and understanding lender. If Folker succeeded, the head of the special assets department would have accomplished exactly what he was asked to do by his superiors. That is, if you are not successful in shoring up the bank's position, get rid of the problem in as gracious a way as possible. The SVP was not upset by Folker's attitude. It was predictable. Within a few weeks, Folker would probably be back and resigned to the fact that the bank's proposal was actually not that bad.

Few, if any, bankers at the time were looking to finance companies that were losing money. And, compared to what the asset-based lenders would be requiring, the bank's proposal was more than competitive. The SVP was not really interested in losing Generipak as a customer. The company's financial condition had not become so bad that it was no longer an acceptable credit risk. However, if the company was not interested in meeting the bank's new requirements, the SVP was prepared to see Generipak leave.

When the time came, Folker agreed to accept the bank's proposal. It took a strong selling job on Hans Monck, and the wives of Generipak's owners, to get them to execute and personally secure the guarantees, but Folker succeeded. He then set about to get the business turned around. Sometimes just coming close to the brink of failure is enough to get good managers to respond effectively and quickly. It worked for Herman Folker and Generipak. A few years after Generipak's brush with financial trouble, he met with the SVP to thank him for being as harsh as he had been.

CHAPTER 4

USING SELF-HELP MEASURES TO GET INFORMAL EXTENSION PROGRAMS FROM UNSECURED CREDITORS

It is a good rule to face difficulties at the time they arise and not allow them to increase unacknowledged.

Edward W. Ziegler

Mr. Ziegler's above shibboleth is especially appropriate for businesses that are adversely impacted by economic changes; particularly, in those cases where such events are combined with a bank or commercial finance company already possessing a validly perfected security interest in the assets of a company. As mentioned previously, the latter situation is occurring with greater and greater frequency; and, given the fragility of the international financial system and widespread political discord, the former could happen at any time. Credit managers are strongly influenced by what they see, read, and hear. When adverse macroeconomic conditions arise, these extenders of credit are more than willing to bend over backward to help a troubled business get through the problems.

Genericoil Energy Services Company, Inc. (Genericoil), is a case in which a business was turned upside down by economic events largely beyond its control. By responding quickly to an industry that changed so abruptly nearly everyone in it was caught by surprise, the owners and managers of Genericoil were able to maintain control of the situation and accomplish the objective of getting suppliers to give the company time to pay a sizable accumulation of old invoices. Of great significance, most of what had to be done was achieved through the efforts of management. Genericoil used outside professionals sparingly; accordingly, the company was able to conserve precious cash.

Genericoil is a privately owned corporation founded in the oilfields of west Texas in 1928 by B. J. Drummand. As a young man, Drummand did what many others had done to earn their stripes in the wild-and-woolly West—roughnecking. He learned early on, though, that the income stream was a lot more certain in the service side of the oil-and-gas business than it was in finding and extracting those commodities.

Drummand discovered he had a knack for doing work as a fisherman—an individual with the ability to deftly "fish" for broken parts, drilling bits, or other debris found in wells deep below the surface. He also found out that if you owned the tools used for fishing, you could earn quite a bit more money by employing other fishermen. Thus was established the predecessor to Genericoil. Drummand's company grew up with the Texas economy; that is, it became a success, albeit having to ride out a few booms and busts.

By the time he retired in the late 1960s, Drummand had built Genericoil into a real powerhouse of a fishing tool company. He was on a first-name basis with many of the CEOs of the leading oil-and-gas companies in the Southwest, and his company was widely regarded as the one you'd call first, if the need arose.

B. J. Drummand handed the reins over to his son, R. Scott Drummand. Scotty, as he was called, was trained at the best schools the state had to offer—some of the finest in the land. He excelled at academics and became a superb administrator. Under his guidance, Genericoil became even more ensconced in its position of leadership in the fishing tool business. He also succeeded in moving Genericoil into manufacturing and machine shops to provide an even broader array of products and services for its customers. Unfortunately, tragedy struck in 1979— Scotty Drummand and his wife were killed in an automobile accident.

Majority ownership and the position of CEO of Genericoil passed to Kelly Drummand—an only child. Kelly was much more inclined to follow in the footsteps of her grandfather than she was to emulate her dad. Kelly was not much of a student, but she did possess a lot of street smarts. At the age of 28, she had already been working at Genericoil for almost 10 years. There was no doubt about who would ultimately run the business; the only question was when. More than a few, in and out of Genericoil, thought Kelly was not quite ready to run a business as big as Genericoil—$18 million revenues in 1980. In Kelly's view, everyone was entitled to an opinion, no matter how stupid and narrow-minded it was!

For three years running, Genericoil posted record revenues and profits. By 1982, the company's annual revenues had surged to $24 million and after tax income hit $580,000. Kelly Drummand, and apparently many others in oil patch, thought the good times would last for some time to come. Recall that the energy states were still prospering for many months after the Northeast and Midwest began suffering through the worst recession since the Great Depression. Kelly's self-confidence was at its peak in those days. Those skeptical about her ability to manage a business like Genericoil were silenced. That is, until the energy world hit the skids.

For Genericoil and Kelly Drummand things began to unravel in early 1983. Revenues that year plummeted to $17.5 million, and the company lost $600,000. Kelly and her management team at Genericoil were slow to initiate expense cuts because they believed the downturn was a temporary aberration. Earlier in the year, the company's superior financial condition and liquidity allowed management to defer making difficult decisions. In late 1983, however, Genericoil's tight cash flow forced Drummand to go to the company's bank to consolidate several smaller loans on individual pieces of equipment and real estate into a single secured term loan. The amount of the loan was $3.5 million. The company granted its lender a security interest in all of its assets. The lender, a big Texas energy bank, was quite comfortable with the fact that it had almost $8 million in assets securing its loan.

The company's fortunes did improve somewhat during 1984. Revenues inched up slightly higher, and Genericoil began to attack operating expenses. The result was a modest profit for the year. The company's lender had a well-secured performing loan, and Genericoil's suppliers were being paid—perhaps not as promptly as some would have liked, but not slow enough to warrant a reduction in credit lines. Genericoil had seemingly escaped from its troubles.

Then came 1985 and 1986. The earlier year was marked by a series of bankruptcies of some of Genericoil's weaker customers. As a result, Genericoil had to write off $574,000 in uncollectible accounts receivable. The competitive environment became even more cutthroat than usual, which compounded the problem. Excess industry capacity and the rush to keep equipment utilization rates up drove prices sharply lower. Some major accounts, which had formerly given Genericoil business on a virtually noncompetitive basis, began to require the company to make razor-sharp bids. The company lost more than $900,000 in 1985. It couldn't get any worse than this, could it? Sure it could.

During the period from November 1985 to August 1986, oil prices made a steep descent from above $31 to approximately $7 a barrel! Genericoil's monthly revenues declined almost as precipitously—from about $1.1 million to $300,000 a month. At that minuscule monthly volume, less than 15 percent of 1982's comparable level of business, the company's net operating losses exceeded its *gross* receipts. Fortunately for Genericoil, the rest of the energy belt was also caught in the crunch.

Everyone understood that the problems were much bigger than any one company. Genericoil used this fact to its distinct advantage. Rather than ignoring its suppliers and other vendors, which by August had collectively extended Genericoil more than $1.6 million in credit, Kelly Drummand decided to make a full disclosure of the company's problems. She spent an entire weekend drafting a letter that would be sent to creditors. With the help of her chief financial officer and the company's outside attorney, who smoothed out a few rough spots, the letter (which appears in Exhibit 4–1) was sent to all creditors as well as employees of Genericoil.

EXHIBIT 4–1
Letter to Creditors Regarding Financial Difficulties

Re: Status of Genericoil's Financial Condition

Dear Creditors:

As you know, oil prices have plunged during the past several months, worsening the already-depressed condition of our industry. The resulting drop in oilfield activity since the first of the year has had an adverse impact on the cash flow of all service companies, including Genericoil. Our company's revenues have fallen to 1970 levels. This is despite the fact that Genericoil's market share has actually risen. We are all experiencing Depressionlike problems.

As a result of forces that are largely outside of our control, we must regrettably inform you that we are not able to handle credit terms as originally agreed. It is vitally important to emphasize that the challenge facing Genericoil is one of liquidity, *not* solvency. Attached is a current balance sheet to demonstrate Genericoil's underlying financial strength. It shows that despite losses incurred in recent years, the company has a solid net worth.

In its long history as a family-owned company, Genericoil has grown to be one of the largest service businesses of its type in Texas, offering a full range of fishing tool, machine shop, and manufacturing products and services. We recognize that Genericoil's success is built upon the support of its creditors. It is our intention to fully honor its obligations to all creditors, once we are in a position to do so.

Following is a brief account of the steps taken thus far by management to address and correct the problems:

1. Continuing reductions in operating expenses have been made in response to previous and anticipated revenue declines.
2. Genericoil's work force has been reduced by more than 60 percent during the past 16 months, both in the field and in administrative areas.
3. An experienced financial team has been assembled to ensure that quality accounting and recordkeeping is maintained.
4. Negotiations have begun with Genericoil's secured lender with the objective of restructuring the credit facility.
5. Longer-range R&D projects and other manufacturing programs have been put on hold pending a better picture for the industry as a whole.
6. A project has been initiated which will identify non-income-producing assets and recommend the best strategies for redeploying or selling them to improve Genericoil's liquidity.
7. Detailed cash flow forecasts are being prepared to enable the company to respond more quickly to conditions in the industry.

In view of the ongoing uncertainty in the oil-and-gas business, these and other steps that management deems to be necessary to improve Genericoil's financial condition will continue. Like many others, we have adopted a busi-

EXHIBIT 4–1 (continued)

ness plan based upon survival. The core assumption underlying our decision to implement the above austerity measures is that no significant improvement will occur in the industry over the immediately foreseeable future. Of course, if the climate changes for the better, we'll be ready to forge ahead.

The changes that have been made, as well as those that are being formulated, will give Genericoil the ability to service all of its current and future obligations. However, the company's cash flow crunch has temporarily stalled its ability to make payments on all of its old debts. Given sufficient time, Genericoil can, and will, honor all past-due obligations.

There are two key ingredients to our achieving our plan. First, we must manage revenues and drive down costs to generate sufficient surplus cash flow to reduce debt on a scheduled basis, while ensuring that all creditors of the same class are treated equitably. Second, with the approval of Genericoil's lending institution, which has a security interest in all of the company's assets, we must find a way to refinance or sell those assets which cannot generate operating cash flow. The cash proceeds will be used to reduce indebtedness or improve liquidity.

As we have assessed the situation, Genericoil should be able to pay old invoices over about a two-year period. We would like to begin making payments on these past-due bills at the rate of 5 percent per month. If you are in agreement with this proposal, please send us a letter of confirmation. It should take about a month to tally your responses. We hope to then begin sending checks within about 60 days. In the interim, we will pay COD for all goods and services needed to do profitable business, provided that price, quality, and terms remain competitive.

Management is resolved that by taking the above steps, the continued viability of Genericoil will be assured and the maximum benefit to all creditors will be realized. The company's secured creditors have shown a strong willingness to support Genericoil during this period of extraordinary industry turmoil. Naturally, the situation is very tenuous and must remain fluid. Our secured lender has made it emphatically clear to us that it will not allow its collateral to be used to make payments on unsecured antecedent debt. In short, Genericoil must operate with positive cash flow if our proposal is to work.

It would only be natural for some of you to be angry with the current state of affairs. We have never had to ask any of our creditors to go along with a deferred payment plan before. But times are tough, and there is little we can do other than request your forbearance. We firmly believe that separate actions by individual unsecured creditors to collect on old invoices will be counterproductive and will result in unnecessary costs to all.

The financial problems of Genericoil are serious; but, to say again, the big issue is one of temporary illiquidity and not of insolvency. Genericoil's management has accepted the challenges and has taken what it thinks are the necessary steps to respond to them. In this highly unsettling situation, we will do whatever is required to ensure the company's continuity and its eventual return to vitality.

The continued support of our company's lender and suppliers as well as

EXHIBIT 4–1 (concluded)

---

our employees and customers is the key to our success in the months ahead. We truly appreciate your understanding and patience in continuing to work with us. Should you have any questions, please call me personally.

I would like to leave you with one final thought. The success of Genericoil through the years has been built upon ethical business practices and the highest level of integrity. These characteristics will form the basis of an even stronger relationship between Genericoil and its creditors in the years ahead as this industry crisis fades from memory. Thank you for your consideration.

Very truly yours,

Kelly Drummand
Chief Executive Officer

Letters such as the one shown in Exhibit 4–1 do have a very powerful impact. For the most part, creditors appreciate hearing from the CEO of a business that is not paying its bills—even when the news is nearly all bad. Without some type of communication from management, individual creditors become worried that they will end up being one of those left holding the bag. Kelly Drummand's letter assuaged the concerns of the great majority of the unsecured creditors to whom it was sent. Genericoil's employees also felt a lot better about the situation.

Although a very high percentage of creditors do respond affirmatively to proposals like the one sent by Genericoil, some creditors simply will not go along with such arrangements. Some companies have very strong credit and collection policies to deal with customers who do not pay their bills when due. They will not accept any excuses or alternatives. Period. Such tactics do work in certain instances but, as we will see a bit further on, not in the case of Genericoil. Shown in Exhibit 4–2 are a few of the less-than-favorable responses Drummand received to her proposal for an informal extension program. She was a little disappointed that her request for more time didn't result in full cooperation, but she was satisfied that a viable out-of-court plan was possible.

EXHIBIT 4–2
Negative Responses to Letter to Creditors

Sample Number 1

Dear Ms. Drummand:

Your indebtedness to the above-referenced creditor has been referred to this collection agency for immediate action. We have obtained copies of all relevant documentation relating to your account with our client and, based upon our analysis, there is no justification for further delay of payment. If your remittance is not received within 10 days, we shall be compelled to take appropriate legal action.

Sample Number 2

Dear Kelly:

We are in receipt of your letter, addressed to the CEO of our company, regarding the proposed 5-percent-per-month solution to the outstanding balance of Genericoil's account with us. We feel your repayment schedule is not adequate. Our counterproposal for the settlement of the debt is for Genericoil to make an immediate payment of 25 percent with the balance due in five equal monthly payments. Please respond to us, in writing, within 10 days. We want to help you get through these difficult times, but we also have to deal with our lenders.

Sample Number 3

Dear Ms. Drummand:

I am an attorney for Universal Van & Storage Company, and I have been instructed to take whatever action may be needed to collect the balance of the tariff charges Genericoil owes to my client. As a regulated motor carrier, Universal is required by law to collect its tariffs in full and may not compromise or forgive these charges. In order to avoid the expense and inconvenience of possible litigation, I very strongly suggest that you pay this debt immediately. If receipt is not made within five days, I will be forced to seek legal remedies on behalf of my client.

Sample Number 4

Dear Madam:

As the representative of the above-named creditor, it is our intention to collect the full amount of the balance owing. Please be advised that if we do not receive payment in five days, we will immediately file a lawsuit to collect the sum due. Upon obtaining judgment, we will proceed with property attachment as provided for under the laws of the State of Texas. If this action becomes necessary, we will ask for court costs, attorney fees, and all other expenses of collection involved. Our future action will be fully controlled by Genericoil's reaction to this notice. YOUR PAYMENT MAILED TODAY WILL PREVENT THIS ACTION.

EXHIBIT 4–2 (*concluded*)

Sample Number 5

Dear Ms. Kelly [sic]:

Please be advised that this office has been retained by the Universal Travel Service Corporation to represent it in the matter of an unpaid claim. Our client has reviewed your proposal and has rejected it as unreasonable. Universal Travel is itself required to pay for all travel vouchers each week, and your failure to pay your bills continues to burden my client's cash flow. In an effort to amicably settle this matter, I have been authorized to permit your company to make six equal monthly payments, together with interest at an annualized rate of 14 percent, and with a junior security interest in accounts receivable. Please respond within 10 business days.

Letters such as those presented in Exhibit 4–2 require a prompt response. The company cannot go along with individualized payment programs if it is to maintain credibility with its other suppliers. Nor will its secured creditor allow junior creditors to get paid with funds representing part of its collateral. A letter such as the one presented in Exhibit 4–3 should get nearly all of the uncooperative creditors to put threats of legal action on hold. If need be, though, a secured creditor can put a stop to all independent legal efforts to collect past-due invoices by actually filing a third-party claim.

EXHIBIT 4–3
Reply to Creditors Threatening Legal Action

Dear Mr. Hartlis:

A short while ago, I wrote to you concerning the cash flow difficulties that we have had at Genericoil. In that letter, I listed the primary reasons for the company's predicament and also mentioned that, while our problems are severe, they are not insolvable. With a little more time and continued support from Genericoil's creditors, we can overcome the temporary cash flow shortfall. A plan to repay general creditors was outlined in that letter and, I am pleased to say, the program was overwhelmingly accepted by the vast majority of those concerned.

Unfortunately, I have just received a notice from your attorney indicating that you do not wish to accept our proposal and that you are considering court action. This was very disappointing to me as it remains my hope to successfully repay all of Genericoil's debts outside the legal arena. To that end, it is essential that creditors refrain from using collection agencies or attorneys to enforce their claims against Genericoil.

EXHIBIT 4–3 (concluded)

I have been advised that because all of the company's assets have been previously pledged to secure the loan from Genericoil's lender, it is virtually certain that unsecured creditors (primarily vendors and suppliers such as your company) will not be able to collect funds through independent legal actions. I'm not a lawyer, but I believe it has something to do with a "third-party claim." I'm told this means that even if you are successful in court, you will not be able to collect on a judgment or a writ of attachment because the secured lender has a preexisting priority claim. I urge you to discuss this matter with knowledgeable counsel before incurring expenses that will not result in tangible benefits.

If Genericoil is not successful in negotiating a plan to repay its creditors out of court, it may have no choice but to file a bankruptcy petition. Such a measure would be highly detrimental to Genericoil's business and would also severely damage your chances of collecting the sum owed to you. Rest assured that I will not seek the court's protection unless all other measures have failed. There simply must be a way for us to resolve this matter equitably. Accepting our proposal for a 20-month payment program is by far a better scenario than any others. Please reconsider your decision and get back to me at your earliest convenience.

Respectfully yours,

Kelly Drummand
Chief Executive Officer

The above program worked for Genericoil. Sometimes having a lone secured creditor can work wonders for a business that gets into trouble. The company's recalcitrant creditors finally agreed to the informal repayment plan. Within a few short months, oil prices rose: first to $15 per barrel, then to an OPEC-set floor of $18, and then to over $20. Genericoil's business slowly got back to profitable levels, and solutions were found to expedite payments to the suppliers and other creditors. By reacting nimbly to the changed economic environment, Genericoil was able to solve its financial troubles by using outside professionals very sparingly. In the process, the company saved itself tens of thousands of dollars. In the next chapter, a less fortunate debtor will need help from specialists in getting creditors to go along with an extension program.

CHAPTER 5

USING PROFESSIONALS TO ASSIST IN OBTAINING FORMAL EXTENSION PROGRAMS FROM UNSECURED CREDITORS

All business proceeds on beliefs, or judgments of probabilities, and not on certainties.

Charles W. Eliot

This chapter deals with a situation in which the owner/manager of a troubled business had no recourse but to use the services of a business turnaround consultant, skilled attorneys, and a specialist from the adjustment department of an affiliate of the National Association of Credit Management (NACM). There was near unanimity of opinion among the creditors of the business that the CEO was unduly optimistic about the future of his operation and, accordingly, was in need of outside help in effectuating a business revitalization program.

The case involves a business named Generituf Carpets, Inc. (Generituf). The company is a retail establishment primarily engaged in the business of selling and installing high-quality carpeting to discriminating customers. A related line of business—draperies—has also become an important part of Generituf's operations. The business was founded in 1968 by Eduardo P. Martee in Miami, Florida. Working long and productive hours, he succeeded in building his first store into a very successful operation. In 1972, the company opened a second store in Coral Gables, an area having Generituf's ideal demographic profile: middle-income families, working spouses, upscale purchasing habits, and growing community. After about eight months of operation, the new store broke into the black and has been a success story ever since.

In 1974, Generituf opened a third store in Pompano Beach. Although it took 14 months, this place of business also reached profitability. In quick succession, three more stores were added. From 1976 to 1979, Generituf experienced its greatest financial success. Sales for 1976 at the six stores were in excess of $6 million, and pretax profits reached nearly $200,000. By 1979, revenues were over $9 million, and pretax profits hit $300,000. Martee thought he had discovered the perfect formula for successful growth.

It would be very difficult for even the sharpest credit analysts to conclude that Generituf's strategic decision making in the latter part of the 1970s was anything other than sound. The company seemed to have developed a solid program for rational growth and expansion. Not surprisingly, lenders and suppliers were eager to provide growth financing for Generituf. In 1980, the company was able to negotiate a $1.5 million unsecured, revolving-credit facility from one of the area's aggressive independent banks. Generituf was also able to expand its aggregate credit lines with its largest carpet mill suppliers by over $500,000.

With substantial new funds available from external sources, as well as strong cash flow from operations, Generituf was ready to grow even more quickly—and to diversify. After extensive demographic, financial, and economic analyses conducted by management and an outside marketing firm, Generituf decided to open a total of six new stores in 1980 and 1981. The company also decided to enter the commercial market for carpeting and related products.

In early 1980, the economic environment in southern Florida was in a state of frenzy. The competition for the best retail store locations was fierce; accordingly, lease rates were extremely high. Generituf was effectively priced out of many of its most desired sites. Instead the company opted for locations with less-than-ideal demographic parameters. In retrospect, the last four stores should not have been located where they were. And the timing of the expansion program proved to be bad. Recall that the early 1980s were a period of very difficult economic times. With the strong performance of its well-established stores, Generituf could have gotten through the recession had it not been for the company's decision to get into commercial markets. Here Generituf made some rather poor credit decisions of its own. The company provided open credit lines to a number of inexperienced and unseasoned developers of office buildings, condominiums, and apartments. In the short run, this resulted in rather sizable increases in revenues and partly obscured the problems arising in the retail side of the business. In the long run, Generituf wrote off $330,000 in uncollectible accounts receivable.

By late 1983, Generituf's suppliers and its bankers realized that some serious problems were not being addressed. Not even Eddie Martee's personal loans to Generituf, which had totaled $125,000 over the previous two years, could stem the tide. A consensus was building that something had to be done with the unprofitable stores. Martee, who still believed in his heart that in the long run things would work out, agreed, albeit reluctantly, to follow the advice of his creditors and retain a consultant to help turn things around.

A highly regarded consulting firm, with many years of experience in retailing, was brought on board in early 1984 to assist in the closing of the four unprofitable stores. Acting on the recommendations of the management consultant, Generituf immediately began negotiations with landlords and arranged lost-our-lease sales to reduce inventory. Within two months the process was completed. The remainder of the inventory, remnants, samples, fixtures, and equipment from the underperforming stores was moved to the profitable ones, and an additional "clearance" sale was held.

The business contraction was accomplished quickly but not without heavy costs: Generituf had to walk away from nearly $250,000 in leasehold improvements; it had $180,000 in fixtures and equipment with little use value and virtually no resale value; and company was still legally liable for the remaining years of the vacated leases. After a series of independent negotiations between Generituf's attorney and legal counsel for the landlords, agreements were reached for settling these claims.

There were three very important considerations in the amicable resolution of the lease matters. First, each store could be re-leased with not too much effort by the landlords. The leasehold improvements made by Generituf could be used by any number of other retail establishments. (The law requires landlords to make bona fide efforts to mitigate the damages they may suffer in these situations.)

Second, Martee had not guaranteed any of the lease payments. Based on the company's strong track record and financial position, he was able to avoid what many lessees cannot. (If he had given his personal guarantee, his personal financial position would probably have been seriously impacted because the landlords would very likely have actively pursued him to recover any deficiencies.)

Third, if Generituf had to resort to using a Chapter 11 bankruptcy proceeding to "reject" the leases, the maximum amounts of the claims available to the landlords would be limited to one year's rent payments plus any unpaid rents prior to Generituf's leaving the premises. In short, the cost for Generituf to vacate the four leases totaled about $130,000.

The cumulative effect of the store closings, bad debt writeoffs, fixed-asset write-downs, and operating losses was that by the end of 1984, Generituf had wiped out its net worth and had a huge working capital deficit. The company was experiencing a severe cash flow crisis, and nearly everyone with a stake in the business knew about it.

As a result of the company's badly weakened financial position, its creditors became deeply concerned about Generituf's survival. In such circumstances, it was not surprising that the company's bank wanted a security interest in all of Generituf's assets as a condition for not calling the loan. Unfortunately, the credit manager of Generituf's largest supplier of carpets—without which the company could not remain in business—threatened to stop shipping if the bank were given such preferential treatment.

Martee was on the horns of a dilemma. In terms of going forward with his business, he had to have carpets and he knew that if his largest supplier decided to withhold shipments, a number of the other carpet mills would take similar actions. Since the bank was not going to advance any new funds, it was of relatively less importance for the future of Generituf. But, if Generituf did not act responsibly, the bank would be left with little choice but to take legal action to enforce its claim. What should he do? Although he was correctly advised that a Chapter 11 bankruptcy petition would place all creditor demands on temporary hold, Martee did not consider this a very palatable alternative. For his type of business, such a step could be suicidal.

The crusty old credit manager who was making Martee's life miserable had a suggestion. Why not contact the head of the adjustment bureau of NACM of Florida to arrange a meeting of creditors to explain the situation? The credit manager was an active member of NACM's national board of directors, and he had seen carpet retailers in other parts of the country successfully use this alternative to the bankruptcy courts. He also said he would be willing to serve as chairperson of a creditors' committee if one were formed.

After meeting for a few hours with the adjustment bureau manager, Martee concluded that this was the alternative he was seeking. He knew, though, that he was treading on unfamiliar turf and needed some help. The adjustment bureau manager gave him the names of three business consultants who had many years of experience in advising companies in such matters. After meeting with each of them, Martee made his choice.

Prior to arranging a general meeting of creditors, the newly formed Generituf negotiating team met several times with the company's bankers and had multiple telephone conversations with the company's eight largest carpet suppliers. Although the bank officers were, at first, adamantly opposed to the idea of participating in an out-of-court reorganization program with the trade creditors, they were savvy enough to realize that such a proposal was clearly preferable to seeing Generituf enter a Chapter 11 proceeding.

As an unsecured creditor, the bank did not have any real leverage in these preliminary negotiations. As the largest individual creditor, the bank would have an influential position in future negotiations, probably as chair or co-chair of the creditors' committee. The turning point came when the carpet mills indicated they would support a continuation of interest payments to the bank during the course of the negotiations. Generituf would also have to agree to pay COD for future carpet orders.

After completing the behind-the-scenes negotiations with the company's most influential creditors, Generituf's managers were almost ready to meet with all of its general creditors to explain the problems it was having and to develop a plan to reorganize the business and repay creditors. To facilitate future negotiations, the business adviser recommended immediately paying off all of Generituf's small creditors. The company had about 50 creditors who were owed $100 or less. Thus, for approximately $3,750, about 40 percent of Generituf's creditors could be paid. Although these payments are technically preferences, they are nearly always a part of any creditor extension plan; so, why not eliminate them before the general meeting?

Although they had previously been slow to act, Martee and his management team became keenly aware of the seriousness of the situation and the company's precarious financial condition. The austerity program instituted during the months preceding the meeting with creditors was indicative of Generituf's determination to survive. Numerous personnel cuts were made, and operating expenses of every kind were slashed from previous levels.

The practical realities of Generituf's situation were such that the company had to operate entirely from internally generated cash flow. Numerous iterations of cash flow forecasts were made, and tough cost-cutting decisions continued until Generituf demonstrated that it could operate on a COD basis with its creditors and stay alive. It is one thing to find a way to bring operating cash receipts and cash disbursements into balance—which Generituf did. It is quite another to figure out how the company can repay all of its antecedent debt.

If Generituf is to repay all of its obligations, which Martee indicated that he fully intends to do, it must do so from future cash flow. The cooperation and forbearance of the company's creditors are obviously integral parts of the success of a turnaround. A complete description of the steps needed to effectuate a business turnaround program are beyond the scope of this book. (Readers might want to refer to a book the author has written on that subject entitled *Revitalizing Your Business.*)

Suffice it to say, Martee, his advisers, his bankers, his suppliers, NACM of Florida, and other interested parties did figure out that it was not only possible but also desirable for Generituf to be restructured so that all of the company's old debts were extended and the company was able to resume profitable operations. Once all of the specifics of the extension agreement were outlined, a law firm specializing in insolvency matters was retained by Generituf to prepare what is called a Creditors' Extension Agreement. Attorneys for the creditors' committee and the bank reviewed the documents, and within a month it was ratified by nearly all of the company's creditors.

Exhibit 5–1, prepared by NACM of Florida, summarizes the repayment plan ultimately approved by Generituf's creditors. Exhibit 5–2 illustrates the consent form that had to be executed by each creditor.

EXHIBIT 5–1
Summary of the Provisions of the Extension Agreement with Creditors

In the matter of

Generituf Carpets, Inc.)	
15267 Dolphin Boulevard)	File:
Miami, FL 33199)	85126
———————————————)	

To the Creditors:

We are pleased to notify you that after several months of negotiations, Generituf's management and advisers have proposed a Creditor's Extension Agreement, which your Creditors' Committee has unanimously agreed should be accepted by all of the company's unsecured creditors.

The complete terms and conditions of Generituf's proposal are contained in the accompanying Creditors' Extension Agreement. We strongly encourage that you read the document in full so that you are well informed of the details of the matter.

To assist you, we have summarized below what we believe are the most pertinent parts of the Creditors' Extension Agreement:

I.   Unsecured creditors, who hold about $3.2 million in claims, are to be paid in full over the life of the agreement. The National Association of Credit Management of Florida will perform as the disbursing agent in accordance with the formula shown in paragraph III below.

II. The management of Generituf believes that the claims of all unsecured creditors will be fully satisfied within five to six years. The exact timeframe is dependent upon the levels of net sales volume and profitability that Generituf is able to achieve. The Creditors' Committee has not been

EXHIBIT 5–1 (*continued*)

able to independently validate the projections presented by management and, thus, it expresses no opinion concerning the length of time that will actually be required for the company to honor the terms of the agreement.

III. The agreement provides for presently unsecured creditors to receive a combination of payments.

    A. Upon acceptance of the repayment plan, as defined more specifically below, Generituf will deposit with NACM of Florida 3 percent of allowed claims, or $100,000, whichever is less. Such funds shall immediately be paid out to creditors.

    B. Generituf will additionally make monthly payments to NACM of Florida in the amount of the following percentages of its net sales—

        (1) 1.0 percent during the first year.

        (2) 1.1 percent during the second year.

        (3) 1.2 percent during the third year.

        (4) 1.4 percent during the fourth year.

        (5) 1.6 percent during the fifth year, and succeeding years until all allowed claims are paid in full.

    C. Generituf will additionally make annual payments equal to 20 percent of its net profits for the preceding fiscal year. The payment will be deposited with NACM of Florida no later than one month after the presentation of financial statements prepared on a "review" basis by an outside CPA firm.

IV. Generituf will grant to NACM of Florida, as trustee for the present unsecured creditors, a security interest in all of its assets. The main purpose of the security interest being granted to present unsecured creditors is to prevent independent actions by dissident creditors and to ensure that the company performs under the plan.

V. There will be no interest payments paid under this agreement to any creditor, except Generituf's bank, which will receive interest payments equal to its average cost of funds.

VI. The $125,000 claim of Eduardo P. Martee, the sole owner and CEO of Generituf, will be subordinate to the claims of the present unsecured creditors and will remain unpaid until all of the old debts of Generituf have been paid in full.

VII. Acceptance of the repayment plan is defined as receipt of affirmative consents from *all* of the unsecured creditors, unless a lower percent is acceptable to the management of Generituf.

VIII. Unsecured creditors will grant general releases [refer to Exhibit 6–1 for details of such a legal document] of any claims they may have against Generituf's sole owner, directors, officers, or employees. The release becomes effective upon acceptance of the repayment plan and the payment by Generituf of the initial deposit described in subparagraph III(A) above. In the event that Generituf subsequently defaults in making payments under the agreement, the only recourse available to unsecured creditors will be enforcing the security interest noted above in paragraph IV.

IX. Unless Generituf's managers and the Creditors' Committee jointly agree,

EXHIBIT 5–1 (*concluded*)

---

      only those creditors who consent to the extension plan will receive funds under the agreement.

  X. In the event that the management of Generituf is not successful in revitalizing the business, and the company subsequently enters a proceeding in a bankruptcy court, the agreement will *not* be deemed to have been accepted for purposes of confirmation under the Bankruptcy Code.

  XI. During the course of the repayment program, the company will provide financial information to the Creditor's Committee and NACM of Florida on a quarterly basis. As noted previously, annual financial statements will also be furnished by Generituf. Periodic bulletins will be sent to all interested parties summarizing the status of the case.

    Enclosed herewith please find a copy of the Consent you will need to complete if you wish to participate in the payment program negotiated on your behalf between Generituf and your Creditors' Committee. We should like to emphasize that your Creditors' Committee has unanimously voted in favor of the proposal. You are urged to sign and return the Ballot as quickly as practicable. No payments can be made until all unsecured creditors have responded. Thank you for your cooperation.

Very truly yours,

Manager
Adjustment
Bureau

enclosures

EXHIBIT 5–2
Consent to Creditors' Extension Agreement

    The undersigned, a creditor of Generituf Carpets, Inc., in consideration for the payments to be made by Generituf to this creditor and other creditors under the Creditors' Extension Agreement (Agreement) dated as of July 14, 1985, executed by Generituf and its Creditors' Committee, in consideration for other consents to be executed by other creditors of Generituf, and for other

EXHIBIT 5–2 (concluded)

good and valuable consideration, hereby consents to the Agreement and agrees to be bound by all of the terms and conditions thereof.

Paragraph III of the Agreement details the amount and the timing of the payments to be made by Generituf to its creditors. The undersigned has read and understands the terms and conditions of the Agreement.

Amount of Claim: $ _____
                              (As of March 27, 1985)

Name of Creditor: _____

Authorized Signature: _____

Address: _____

                         _____ ZIP _____

Date: _____-_____-_____

Please complete and return this Consent form in the enclosed envelope to the Adjustment Bureau of NACM of Florida. Time is of the essence in this matter, so please respond as quickly as practicable.

The impact on Generituf's capital structure was that $3.2 million of short-term liabilities were converted to long-term debt. The company still had an intolerably great debt-to-worth ratio, but its working capital position was greatly improved. A definitive program established for debt reduction was pegged to revenues in addition to future profits. Thus, so long as Generituf remains in business there will be funds paid to creditors. The formerly unsecured creditors also benefited in that they now have a security interest in Generituf's assets. This means that in the event the situation does not improve as planned and the company subsequently fails, these creditors have some assurance that their claims will have some value in a liquidation.

Although the repayment program could prove too onerous, Eddie Martee was satisfied that he had gone the limit in trying to rectify matters. The moral of this story is that when a business and its creditors work together to find a solution to financial problems, they can accomplish wonders.

CHAPTER 6

GETTING UNSECURED CREDITORS TO COMPROMISE, OR TAKE LESS THAN, THE FULL AMOUNT OWED THEM

A bird in hand is worth two in the bush.

Cervantes

Creditor confidence in the competency of the managers running a troubled business is of crucial importance for a successful long-term workout. But, as stated previously, it is a popular notion that managers tainted with having been associated with problems aren't perceived as capable of satisfactorily identifying them, let alone correcting them. What happens when certain creditors have deep-rooted feelings that the current management is lacking in the qualities needed for effective action? Sometimes the absence of trust in managers' business judgments can work to their very great advantage. In cases of grave financial difficulty, the chance to receive a cash settlement for less than the amount owed is sometimes readily accepted by creditors. The impact on the ailing business's balance sheet can be very substantial.

Generican Distribution Company, Inc. (Generican), illustrates just how effective a recapitalization program this can be. The company was founded in Chicago in 1952 by Sean Mc-Clernan, an enterprising, confirmed bachelor who had spent several years working in sales for one of the major U.S. can manufacturing companies. He recognized a need that was not being very well served—supplying a wide variety of cans to the growing number of small businesses whose orders were not large enough to warrant a direct sales call by his company or the other large can manufacturers.

McClernan was actually able to set up his business with the blessing and help of his previous employer. His former sales manager saw real talent in McClernan and, though he did not want to see McClernan leave, reasoned that McClernan would probably be of great help in boosting sales of products he knew best. McClernan's old boss was quite right. In the early stages of Generican's development, McClernan was more a manufacturer's rep than an independent distributor.

As he grew more experienced with the market, McClernan discovered that his prior company's product lines were not adequate to fill all of his customers' needs. So, McClernan set out to expand his base of suppliers. Since in nearly all of the cases this did not represent a direct competitive threat, he was able to remain in the good graces of his principal supplier as well as expand his network. Over the next few decades, McClernan skillfully used his growth strategies to build a business that distributed nearly every type of metal and plastic container manufactured in the United States. He also forged solid relationships with all of the country's major container makers.

Over the years, the company had gradually established five sales offices in key midwest cities. Except for a small percent of sales—which, in accordance with Generican's instructions, were direct-shipped by the container manufacturers to Generican's customers—all of the distribution of container products was made from the company's warehouse and headquarters in Chicago. McClernan had decided many years before that Generican should build its own distribution center. In 1971, the company obtained interim construction financing from one of Chicago's best-known banks and later obtained a fixed-rate mortgage from a large New York-based insurance company.

By 1977, Generican's annual sales had increased to $10 million, and after tax profits were a respectable $250,000. By all accounts, the company was a winner. As the sole owner, Sean McClernan was doing very nicely indeed. He was paying himself $123,000 a year and had all the other perks and trappings of a self-made millionaire. What else was there for McClernan to accomplish in the container distribution business? Not much, in the short run, so he decided to sell the company and move to sunny California and play golf. For the previous six years, he had been taking an annual month-long vacation in Palm Springs to escape some of Chicago's winter cold.

How much was Generican worth, and to whom could he sell it? McClernan didn't have a clear idea but thought he knew where to find the answer. He called his account officer at his bank. The banker suggested that if McClernan were serious about selling he really ought to have Generican valued by an independent valuation firm. The banker referred him to one of the leading appraisal companies in town. Within a month, these valuation specialists presented a report showing that Generican, in their opinion, was worth $1.8 million. Several different methods were used to arrive at the fair market value of the business, so McClernan felt comfortable with the number. The value represented a premium of about $300,000 over Generican's net book value, but then the warehouse was carried at depreciated historical cost. With this adjustment, the numbers made a lot of sense.

After discussing the subject with a few close friends, owners of other medium-sized businesses as well as his professional advisers, McClernan, always slightly ahead of his time, decided he would offer to sell Generican to the company's senior managers, three of whom had been with McClernan for 10 or more years. The only problem was that none of them had much of a personal net worth. The concept of a leveraged buyout (LBO, as it is widely known today) had only recently begun to blossom, but it seemed an eminently sensible idea to McClernan. Generican's managers were greatly interested in pursuing the opportunity.

Where should McClernan and his cohorts start to arrange an LBO? At the bank, of course. Although Generican's account officer was very much supportive of the company and could easily arrange a working capital credit facility, she knew that an LBO could not get financed through her corporate banking group, which was not equipped to handle asset-based lending. The bank had recently formed a new unit, though, to do more highly leveraged transactions. Introductions were quickly arranged with the bank's commercial finance subsidiary. It took very little time for the credit officers of this lender to see a lot of potential.

In less than three weeks, the asset-based lender's audit and credit review team finished its analysis. Generican was organized around a group of good managers (although none could quite measure up to the soon-to-retire McClernan). After tax earnings were consistently in the 2-to-3-percent range for the prior five years. The debt/worth ratio was 1.2/1.0. Internal controls and accounting systems were in place. Accounts receivable were clean. Inventory was free of slow-moving goods. The machinery and equipment was in good operating condition. And the warehouse was well maintained. In short, Generican was an excellent candidate for an LBO.

After another three weeks of intensive discussion and analysis between and among Generican's prospective new CEO, other key company managers, and the asset-based lender's senior officers, a financing proposal was made to Generican. In summary, the lender would be able to grant Generican a six-year term loan for the purpose of acquiring all of Sean McClernan's common stock. The interest rate on the loan would be pegged at prime plus two and one-quarter percent, floating. The loan was expected to be repaid from the future earnings of the company. In consideration for the loan, all of Generican's presently unencumbered assets would be subject to a first-priority blanket lien by the lender. In addition, the new owners would be required to invest a minimum of $100,000, personally guarantee the loan, and secure the guarantees with second mortgages on their residences.

The maximum amount of the loan would equal: 80 percent of eligible accounts receivable; plus 40 percent of qualified inventory; plus 65 percent of the under-the-hammer appraised value of machinery and equipment; plus 60 percent of the market value of the warehouse; *minus* any previously existing liens on the assets. The formula resulted in Generican being able to offer $1.2 million to McClernan in cash and the remainder, $600,000, in a six-year, fully amortizing secured note that would be specifically subordinated to the bank's claims but senior to the claims of unsecured creditors. (These latter creditors did not know many of the details of the transaction, but they would find out a few years later.) The lender considered the subordinated note as the functional equivalent of equity. The interest rate on the deferred portion of the payment to McClernan would be fixed at 8 percent per annum.

Generican's first full year under new ownership, 1979, was the best year in the company's history. Sales reached $12.8 million, and after tax profits were $210,000—not bad, considering the company paid the bank and Sean McClernan almost $160,000 in interest. In addition, $300,000 in term debt was repaid. Everyone connected with the business was happy with the way things were working. The new stockholders had earned a return on their invested capital of 210 percent in one year! McClernan lowered his golf handicap to plus 12. The bank's commercial finance subsidiary was so pleased that it placed a "tombstone" advertisement in one of America's leading business publications, telling other privately owned businesses interested in doing an LBO to seek out its advice and financing.

It was a different story altogether in 1980. The prime rate zoomed to double digits and didn't stop until it hit 20 percent. All of a sudden the cash flow scenario on which the LBO was based was invalidated. Sales did hit a peak of $13.2 million, but profits dropped to a scant $25,000. Generican met its interest obligations from operating cash flow but had difficulty meeting the principal payments. To satisfy its debt service requirements, the company had to lean on its vendors. Stretching out accounts payable in that period of economic turmoil was not difficult. Everyone, it seemed, had problems adjusting to surging interest rates. And many, many people thought the problems were only temporary. They certainly weren't for Generican.

During 1981 and 1982, the early years of Reaganomics, the interest rate gyrations didn't begin to stabilize until they had reached more than 22 percent. Generican was severely impacted by the recession. In 1981, it lost $180,000 on $12.1 million in sales. In 1982, the company lost another $250,000 on sales of $10.7 million. During a 21-month period, Generican twice had to go to its lender and request a reduction in principal payments. The lender initially consented to temporarily reduce the annual principal payments to $100,000.

As the losses mounted and Generican's cash flow was strained to the breaking point, the lender stopped requiring the principal payments, relying on the fact that it had adequate coverage for its loan. McClernan's principal and interest payments, however, had to be suspended entirely in order for the lender to agree to Generican's requests. McClernan did not want to be the one to force his former mates into an irreversible financial bind; so, ignoring the proper advice of his legal counsel, he agreed to go along.

Generican's owners tried everything they could to solve the company's financial difficulties, but nothing seemed to work. The slide toward a bankruptcy petition gathered momentum when a couple of savvy credit managers at important suppliers finessed management into paying some fairly sizable old invoices by threatening to instigate legal action if their claims were not paid. The loan officers of the asset-based lender were very upset by this action because they believed management should have convinced those unsecured suppliers to wait for their payments.

The best that an unsecured creditor should be able to do in a developing financial crisis is to get in line behind a secured creditor. To do that the unsecured creditor must file the lawsuit, win a judgment, obtain a writ of attachment, and attempt to execute it. Having done all that, the unsecured creditor must still deal with the fact that a third party stands ahead of it. In the event of a liquidation, unsecured creditors will only get paid if all of the priority and secured claims are satisfied.

The decision to pay some of the old debts of some suppliers, when the company had only recently gotten the asset-based lender to extend the time to repay the principal on its loan, caused the lender's credit officers to lose confidence in Generican's managers. The lender strongly suggested that the company consider getting a financial adviser to help solve its troubles. The lender gave Generican the names of four financial consultants who it thought could be of assistance.

The owners/managers of Generican spent a few days thinking about the lender's recommendation, and then they acted. They retained a financial consultant specializing in crisis management. In less than a week, the business adviser concluded that something had to be done quickly if Generican was to avoid filing Chapter 11. What she found was that in addition to the asset-based lender's debt (about $800,000) and the McClernan note ($400,000), trade and other unsecured vendor credit amounted to $1.2 million. And a number of these latter creditors had actually commenced legal proceedings or had sent the unpaid invoices to collection agencies or attorneys. She urged Generican's managers to convene a general meeting of creditors as soon as possible so that the company could tell its story. They agreed. The business consultant arranged a meeting for two weeks hence, through the Chicago-Midwest Credit Management Association.

At the meeting, a full disclosure was made of Generican's financial predicament. The unsecured general creditors in attendance received relatively few surprises. Like so many other companies who had pledged all of their assets to secured creditors, Generican had little to offer other creditors. A liquidation analysis prepared by Generican's financial staff and the business adviser indicated that if the company ceased operations, the secured creditors (including Sean McClernan) and priority claimants would be paid in full and unsecured claimants would be lucky to get eight cents on the dollar. (Since more than a year had passed, McClernan was no longer considered an insider as defined by the bankruptcy court.) Not surprisingly, the unsecured general creditors agreed to cooperate with Generican while it worked out a plan to repay its debts. A creditors' committee was formed to review the facts of the case and, hopefully, get something for their fellow suppliers.

After a few weeks of reviewing Generican's financial books and records, the creditors agreed that virtually nothing would be left for unsecured creditors if the company failed. What could be done? A five-year extension program? It was very unlikely that a long-term repayment program would work because Generican could barely make the interest payments on its debt to the asset-based lender, and the company was already in arrears to McClernan for past-due principal and interest. A radical change in Generican's capitalization was needed. Perhaps some of the debt could be converted to equity. And perhaps the unsecured creditors would accept less than the full amount owed if they were offered a cash settlement. But who would be interested in funding such a program? The asset-based lender wasn't interested. It was comfortable with the fact that it would get all of its money back, irrespective of which course of action Generican pursued.

It turns out that Sean McClernan held the key. After almost three years of retirement and enough golf to be quite satisfied, he was ready to get back into the fray. The prospect of helping rescue the company he built had a lot of appeal to him. At 63, he believed he still had plenty of managerial mileage left. Most important of all, he had the financial wherewithal to effectuate a viable plan to recapitalize Generican. He had kept most of the funds from selling Generican in very liquid investments—blue-chip stocks, high-grade corporate bonds, and Treasury securities. Therefore, he could convert some of those investments into cash on short notice. Additionally, he didn't need the $400,000 still owed to him from Generican. For the right consideration, he would be willing to convert that debt to equity.

After several weeks of negotiation, McClernan and his legal and financial advisers were able to get Generican's owners to agree to sell 80 percent of the company back to him. McClernan wanted to retain his key managers and felt a continuing ownership position would be a vital part of the turnaround plan. The only consideration required of McClernan was that he would substitute his personal guarantee for theirs with the asset-based lender. Since the owners/managers faced the prospect of losing not only their investments in Generican but also their residences if the company went belly-up, they reluctantly agreed. The lender was pleased to see that McClernan would be returning to Generican, and, since the guarantees of the current owners were of dubious value anyway, the lender consented to the arrangement.

Next, McClernan and his negotiating team met with the creditors' committee to get those individuals to agree to recommend acceptance of a cash payment offer of 25 percent of the amount owed. (To inject the spirit of compromise and flexibility into the negotiations, the initial offer was 20 percent; the committee countered with 30 percent; and the desired figure of 25 percent was achieved.) Since the cash payment offer was three, or more, times greater than the unsecured creditors would probably receive in a liquidation of Generican, the creditors' committee unanimously recommended acceptance of McClernan's proposal. To ensure that no problems would surface at a later date, each unsecured creditor had to enter into a binding agreement. Exhibit 6–1 presents a sample of the agreement that was finally negotiated with each unsecured general creditor. All of the unsecured creditors were required to separately execute the agreement prior to receipt of payment.

EXHIBIT 6–1
Sample Compromise Agreement and Release of Claims

This Agreement and Release of Claims (hereinafter Agreement) is entered into by and between Generican Distribution Company, Inc. (hereinafter Generican), and Zefco Container Mfg. Co., Inc. (hereinafter Releasor). Generican and Releasor are collectively referred to as "the parties."

Background

Generican is presently experiencing severe financial problems. As a result of these business troubles and the adverse impact they have had on Generican's cash flow and overall financial condition, the parties acknowledge that Generican's ability to pay the full amount of debt due to Releasor is extremely uncertain. Furthermore, the existence of the obligations threaten Generican's ability to operate.

Accordingly, the payment noted herein below in section 1 (Payment) will be the only payment made on the indebtedness itemized on the invoices that Generican and Releasor have mutually agreed are owing. An attachment is included specifying the exact amount of the claims to be satisfied as a result of the agreement. In Zefco's case, the gross amount of the claims is $12,860.

The funds to be paid to the unsecured general creditors of Generican will be made available by Sean McClernan. He is the former owner of Generican and, upon completion of the Agreement, will become the majority owner, holding 80 percent of the common stock of Generican. As a matter of interest, Mr. McClernan has agreed to convert all of the amount owing to him by Generican to equity.

Agreement

In consideration of the following terms, covenants, and conditions, the parties agree as follows:

1. *Payment.*
   Upon the satisfaction of all of the conditions set forth in this Agreement, Generican shall cause to be delivered to Releasor a check payable to Releasor in the amount of $3,215 in full and complete satisfaction of the undisputed claims listed in the schedule attached hereto.

EXHIBIT 6–1 (*continued*)

2. *Release of Claims.*
   [This is fairly standard legal language for obtaining a General Release. It covers just about everyone ever connected to the transaction. It was prepared by McClernan's lawyers.]
   (*i*) Releasor, on behalf of itself and its affiliates, principals, officers, directors, agents, servants, stockholders, employees, attorneys, insurers, representatives, partners, joint venturers, assigns, heirs and successors, hereby releases and forever discharges Generican and its affiliates, principals, officers, directors, agents, servants, stockholders, employees, attorneys, insurers, representatives, partners, joint venturers, assigns, heirs and successors and all persons acting by, through, under, or in concert with the released parties. . . .
   (*ii*) Releasor knowingly and voluntarily waives any and all rights that it has or may have, or its affiliates have or may have, under the provisions of the laws of the State of Illinois. Generican acknowledges that a General Release does not extend to claims which the Releasor does not now know or suspect to exist in its favor at the time of executing the release, which if known by the releasor must have materially affected its settlement with the released parties. Notwithstanding the foregoing, Releasor acknowledges and agrees that this waiver is an essential and material term of this Agreement, without which the document would not have been executed.
3. *Indemnity and Attorneys' Fees.*
   Releasor agrees that if it or any of its affiliates hereafter commence any action arising out of, based upon, or relating to any claims released hereunder and if the released parties are made party to said suit, the Releasor shall defend the released parties and shall pay to them, in addition to any damages caused to them, attorneys' fees incurred by them in defending or otherwise responding to such suit or claim.
4. *Legal Defense.*
   This General Release may be pleaded as a full and complete defense to, and may be used as the basis for an injunction against, any action, suit, or other proceeding instituted, prosecuted or attempted in breach of the terms of this Agreement.
5. *Warranty of Authority.*
   Releasor warrants and represents that it has not heretofore assigned or transferred or purported to assign or transfer to any person not a party hereto, any released matter or any portion thereof. Releasor agrees to indemnify and hold harmless the released parties from and against any claim based on or in connection with or arising out of any assignment or transfer or purported or claimed assignment or transfer.
6. *Different Facts.*
   The parties agree that if the facts with respect to this Agreement are found hereafter to be different from the facts they now believe to be true, the parties expressly accept and assume the risk of such possible difference in facts and hereby agree that this General Release is and will remain effective irrespective of such difference in facts.

EXHIBIT 6–1 (*concluded*)

In witness whereof the parties have executed this Agreement as of the day set forth by their signature.

Date: _____

_____
Releasor(s)

Date: _____

_____
Generican Distribution Company, Inc.

By: _____

The Chicago-Midwest Credit Management Association agreed to act as the escrow agent to ensure that the terms and conditions were met before funds were disbursed. McClernan made a $300,000 refundable deposit to the NACM affiliate to seal the deal. The creditors almost unanimously approved the offer. It was decided that the dollar amount owing to the claimants who did not go along with the offer was so small that the parties felt the risk was well worth assuming. The notice shown in Exhibit 6–2, accompanied by a check equal to 25 percent of the amount owing to the payee, was sent to each unsecured creditor of Generican.

EXHIBIT 6–2
Closing Bulletin Regarding Compromise Agreement with Unsecured Creditors

In the matter of

Generican Distribution Company, Inc.) File: 84013
12277 Lakeshore Drive) Final Communication—
Chicago, IL 60699) Case Now Closed
)
_____)

EXHIBIT 6-2 *(concluded)*

To the Creditors:

We are very pleased to inform you that after three months of negotiations between your Creditors' Committee and the representatives of Generican, an agreement has been reached and a settlement has been formulated. The proposal was unanimously recommended by your Creditors' Committee and overwhelmingly approved by more than 95 percent of all unsecured creditors of Generican.

To reiterate the salient parts of the agreement, Generican offered, and the unsecured creditors accepted, a proposal for a cash payment equal to 25 percent of the amount of the unsecured claims against the company. You will recall that the Creditors' Committee, after evaluating all of the available information, concluded that the proposal was the best means of maximizing recovery for creditors holding unsecured claims.

The Creditors' Committee considered the liquidation value of Generican and, based on the secured position of the company's lenders, concluded that closure of Generican and conversion of assets to cash would result in a payment to unsecured creditors of less than 10 percent—only about one third of the cash amount offered by Generican through Mr. McClernan. Thus, it was apparent that the Generican proposal was in the best interest of all unsecured creditors.

Our check in your favor representing 25 percent of the principal amount of your undisputed, unsecured claim is enclosed herewith. Please take note that the check bears a restrictive endorsement. Upon the clearing of the item through our demand deposit account at our bank you will have affirmed your agreement to accept the payment in full settlement of your claim against Generican Distribution Company, Inc., as provided for in the Agreement and Release of Claims document that you previously executed.

The administration of the case is now being brought to a fruitful conclusion. It is appropriate to acknowledge the substantial efforts made by your Creditors' Committee in negotiating what all involved believe to be a fair and equitable settlement. Without the contributions of the Creditors' Committee, it is doubtful that Generican could have achieved the results that were produced.

Thank you for allowing us to be of service in this matter.

Very truly yours,

Manager
Adjustment Bureau

encl. (1 check)

The impact of the recapitalization program on Generican was enormous. McClernan's $400,000 note was converted to equity. The $1.2 million in claims of unsecured creditors was satisfied in full with the payment of $300,000 in cash. The difference, $900,000, was forgiven. The after tax benefit to Generican was more than $600,000. The company was transformed from one having a small, negative net worth to one with nearly $1 million in net worth. By freeing itself of such a large amount of indebtedness, Generican was able to quickly turn its attention to solving the remaining business problems. Over the next few years, Generican was able to return to profitable operations, qualify for trade credit, and resume making payments on the asset-based lender's debt. By the end of 1987, the company was able to obtain bank financing again. Some stories do have a happy ending.

CHAPTER 7

NEGOTIATING AN OUT-OF-COURT REORGANIZATION PLAN WITH CONFIRMATION IN BANKRUPTCY COURT

> Small opportunities are often the beginning of great enterprises.
>
> *Demosthenes*

This chapter deals with a business that gets into such extraordinarily deep financial trouble it has to resort to using a highly structured out-of-court reorganization program, which then needs to be confirmed by a bankruptcy court—a process that can take just a few months rather than the years a typical bankruptcy case requires. Although it is desirable to utilize the services of attorneys, consultants, and other turnaround professionals as sparingly as possible, their use sometimes cannot be avoided. In those instances, it is far preferable to save viable businesses, even at the attendant high costs, than allow them to fail.

Generilou Oil Recycling Co., Inc. (Generilou), illustrates this recapitalization technique. Generilou is a Louisiana-based energy concern founded by Luke Ruston in 1973. The company's original business purpose, however, was not recycling oil; it was refining oil. And even the latter activity was more accidental than intentional. The story really begins in 1968, when Ruston opened the first of his successful chain of 40 gasoline service stations in Louisiana. In 1972, he bought an outdated refinery primarily because it had sizable gasoline storage facilities, not because it had refining potential. The financing package was very attractive as well: a $500,000 price, 10 percent down, and the balance over 12 years at 6 percent interest with a $100,000 balloon payment. Good fortune seemed once again to smile on Ruston.

In 1973, the Emergency Petroleum Allocation Act was passed. This was one measure the U.S. government used to deal with the energy crisis that erupted when OPEC caused the price of oil to rise suddenly and unexpectedly. The legislation had the effect of granting artificial price advantages to small independent refiners. The purpose was to increase the country's capacity to produce and refine domestic crude oil. Luke Ruston thought this was the opportunity of a lifetime. He quickly sold his gasoline service stations to one of the major oil companies, and he began developing plans to put the proceeds to work in rebuilding the refinery.

In 1974, Mitch Reese, another talented entrepreneur who had developed a profitable waste oil trucking company, joined forces with Luke Ruston. They shared a common view that with the government as a prime mover, the day of the independent refiner had arrived. Not the least bit bashful, together they formulated a plan to build Generilou into a vertically integrated refiner and distributor of a number of petroleum products, including jet fuel, gasoline, motor oil, fuel oil, and asphalt.

Their first step was to rebuild or replace much of the existing refinery. Ruston and Reese not only personally financed most of the project but also got their hands dirty by helping out in various phases of the construction. Although they already had a good feel for the business, they literally wanted to be involved in and understand its every facet. Between 1974 and 1976, Generilou's owners spent almost $4 million to restore the refinery to operating condition. (It would now cost about four times that much to do the same thing.) The result of their efforts was a refinery capable of processing 15,000 barrels of crude oil per day. Additionally, storage capacity for pre- and post-refined products was expanded to 200,000 barrels.

It might seem to the reader that Ruston and Reese were a trifle carried away by the spirit of patriotism, but they were proud that Generilou was ready to take its place among the independent refiners in helping the United States overcome its dependence on foreign oil. To say the company was successful in its initial endeavors is an understatement. Revenues from the refinery grew from just $8 million in 1976 to $111 million in 1981! The primary stimulus for this phenomenal growth was something called the Entitlements Program, another part of the massive 1970s effort in this country to develop increased energy self-sufficiency. The U.S. government gave the small independent refiners an artificial pricing advantage vis-à-vis the major oil companies, allowing them to obtain enough crude oil to keep their refineries running on a productive and profitable basis.

As well as the company was doing, Ruston and Reese knew the competitive advantage that Generilou and the other independents enjoyed would not last forever. They concluded that when, not if, the decontrol of prices for domestically produced crude oil became a reality, Generilou had better have a more broadly based business to cushion the blows that the majors were sure to deliver. In the absence of price supports, the independents would be hard pressed to compete with the country's large refiners because the latters' economies of scale permit them to obtain and process crude at lower unit costs and to sell the finished products at lower prices.

To avoid the prospect of competing head to head with the major refiners, Generilou management began to search for a unique market niche in the energy industry in late 1978. The company decided to convert a portion of its refining capacity to recycling waste oil into fuel oil. Over the next few years, Generilou evolved into one of the largest purchasers of used crankcase oil in the region.

Ruston and Reese invested a considerable amount of their time (before they invested their money) in developing expertise in the oil-recycling industry. Reese, you'll recall, had been tangentially involved in the business as a result of his previous venture in the waste oil trucking business. They became aware that a considerable amount of money and effort had already been expended by other organizations—some of them quite large—in attempting to recycle waste oil into a lube oil base stock that was the qualitative equivalent to virgin lube oil base stock.

Technologies were in existence to accomplish that end. However, the predominant recycling processes in use left a high residue, about 25 percent of the original feedstock, of extremely hazardous substances that must be disposed of in specially designed landfills. Generilou's entrepreneurial owners were interested in developing a recycling process that produced virtual 100 percent efficiency; that is, it solved the problem of hazardous by-product as well as produced high-quality lube oil base stock. This kind of thinking has advanced technologies since the dawn of history. All it takes is money, and Generilou had a lot of that running through the business.

In early 1981, at about the same time Generilou was shifting its emphasis from refining crude oil to recycling waste oil, it developed an association with an energy consulting firm that was close to completing a design for a process to achieve a 100 percent throughput of recycled waste oil. To Messrs. Ruston and Reese, it seemed like a stroke of Providence. Over the next two years, Generilou invested (what turned out to be) in excess of $5.1 million dollars in a desperate financial gamble to develop the consultants' ideas into a viable business enterprise. With better timing and a little luck, things might have worked out sans the financial intrigue. But, of course, they didn't.

One of President Reagan's first official acts on taking office in early 1981 was to dismantle the energy programs set up during the Ford and Carter administrations. As Generilou's management knew would happen, without price supports the economics for virtually all independent refiners soon became disadvantageous. But no one in the industry was quite prepared for the swiftness or the severity of the Reagan administration's implementation program. Most people thought that a phase-out period on price controls would be granted to ease the return to more orderly markets. That didn't happen.

The adverse impact on Generilou's operating performance was exacerbated by the fact that the company was deeply committed to developing its recycling technology. The next two years were a period of dramatic adjustments in the company's financial condition. Although they were aware that trying to retain a share of the refinery market was probably a losing battle, they could not simply let that side of the business slide into oblivion. They needed the refinery's cash flow to finance the completion of the new process for converting waste oil to recycled lube oil base stock. Everything else had to take a back seat to the future salvation of Generilou.

The technological transformation of Generilou from a relatively minor entry in the oil refinery industry into a potentially major recycler of waste oil was essentially completed in early 1984. The cost of remaking Generilou into a different kind of company was very, very great. The combination of operating losses in the refinery and the development costs in the recycling business venture resulted in huge losses in the 1982–84 period. After Generilou's outside accountants completed their annual audit, the bottom line was that Generilou had a net worth of *minus $3 million* at the end of 1984. The company had reached a state of ultimate illiquidity. Access to external capital was unavailable at any cost, and creditors were demanding payments on past-due accounts. Generilou was on the verge of having to file a bankruptcy petition to stave off angry creditors.

Generilou's general counsel suggested to Ruston and Reese that the time had come to seek advice from a law firm specializing in insolvency matters. Acting on the advice of several of their friends in the refinery business who themselves had gotten into difficult financial straits, Ruston and Reese went to Houston to meet with an attorney who had a substantial amount of experience in the reorganization business. Houston also happened to be the headquarters city of Generilou's largest creditor, a subsidiary of a major oil company.

After they explained their story as fully as they could in three hours, the attorney said he thought there was an outside chance that Generilou could avoid filing bankruptcy—at least for the time being. But they would have to arrange to meet with their creditors soon to explain Generilou's financial problems and their plan to resolve past-due accounts.

That same afternoon, a hastily arranged meeting took place with the manager of the adjustment bureau of the Houston Association of Credit Management (HACM). It was decided at HACM that an out-of-court program had a chance to work. A general meeting of Generilou's 325 creditors was then scheduled for 10 days following HACM's receipt of the names and addresses of all Generilou's open accounts payable. This data was provided by overnight delivery the next day, and HACM had its Bulletin No. 1 (a notice to Generilou's creditors concerning the date, place, time, and purpose of the meeting) in the mail that evening.

The 10 days flew by all too quickly for Messrs. Ruston and Reese. (The feeling must be somewhat akin to awaiting trial.) With the help of a business consultant recommended by the insolvency lawyer, Generilou's owners had prepared a well-written market analysis and business plan which they thought clearly demonstrated that Generilou's future was in recycling waste oil into lube oil base stock and then, after blending in the appropriate additives, marketing a wide range of automotive and industrial lubricants. The venture not only had financial potential but was also a socially responsible activity. Preserving scarce natural resources such as petroleum products had a high national priority (at least back then it did).

Although they were well coached by their advisers and the presentation was well made, the meeting with the roomful of increasingly hostile creditors did not go well. Ruston and Reese thought their scenario for having Generilou become a major recycler of waste oil made all the sense in the world. Generilou's eight largest creditors, unfortunately, turned out to be either independent brokers of crude oil or major companies. And *they* didn't really give a damn about recycling waste oil! While the Generilou financial saga was being told, those creditors—to a person, it would later come out—could only relate to the fact that they had unwittingly "financed" the new Generilou venture.

In a private meeting of creditors immediately following the presentation by Generilou's representatives, the consensus was that the creditors had been taken. They were livid at the thought that they were never informed about the decisions to radically alter the nature of Generilou's business. They were downright distraught when told that over about a three-year period, Generilou's combined accounts receivable and inventory had plunged from more than $14 million to less than $1 million, while accounts payable only dropped from about $12 million to just over $8 million.

In short, Generilou had virtually no liquid assets with

which to satisfy creditor claims. The principal remaining asset was a waste oil recycling facility. The value of this mass of specially configured concrete and metal was open to wide speculation. Its approximately $5 million book value would certainly be greatly diminished under any liquidation scenario. It would take someone familiar with the technology to see any future value in the facility.

The creditors wanted vengeance. The suggestion of an immediate involuntary Chapter 7 bankruptcy petition was offered more than once. It would teach those deceptive characters a lesson they would never forget. Regrettably, as some of the cooler heads observed, it would also result in little, perhaps no, recovery for the creditors. It is not easy for a credit manager to report to his or her superiors that a full charge-off is necessary. Better to exhaust all the possibilities than give in to temporary anger.

Generilou's special counsel had carefully pointed out that the estimated liquidation value of the company's remaining assets (primarily the scant receivables, inventory, and the refinery itself) would only provide about $1.5 million in cash (after costs of liquidation were deducted) compared to the more than $13 million in total claims against the company. And the mortgage holder on the property had first priority claim for about $200,000, leaving about $1.3 million for the unsecured creditors of Generilou.

The approximately 10 percent recovery on unsecured claims indicated above was under ideal circumstances. As a practical matter, Generilou would certainly seek an immediate conversion of the involuntary Chapter 7 to a Chapter 11 debtor-in-possession case. The realities of today's legal world are such that bankruptcy judges almost invariably grant these requests, particularly when businesses are represented by a lawyer with a reputation like that of Generilou's attorney.

In a Chapter 11 case, Generilou would probably attempt to find an asset-based lender to advance funds on a superpriority basis—with the court's approval. This means the new lender would be the first to receive any funds in a liquidation. Without a doubt, the lenders who engage in this specialized type of financing have an excellent understanding of how much they can safely lend and get back under the worst case.

The bottom line for Generilou's unsecured creditors was that if the company's management aggressively fought in court to remain in control of Generilou, there would likely be quickly escalating administrative costs, further dissipation of assets, and, ultimately, a recovery closer to zero than the approximately 10 percent noted. As distasteful as it was, the owners of Generilou had gotten the company into such deep trouble that the creditors had little choice but to try and figure out how to get some of their money back out of the future cash flows.

As the day came to a close, the following agreements were reached between Generilou and its unsecured creditors:

1. A temporary moratorium on all unsecured debt was granted for a period of 90 days.
2. A creditors' committee was formed to monitor the business and seek to negotiate a repayment plan.
3. Generilou would give present suppliers the first opportunity to do business with the company, so long as price, quality, and service remained competitive.
4. Generilou would pay COD for all purchases of goods and services during the moratorium period.
5. No creditors would receive any payments on their prior claims, except as a result of an overall repayment program that remained to be negotiated by the creditor's committee.
6. The creditors' committee would receive, within the next two weeks: (*i*) copies of Generilou's annual financial statements for the past four years; (*ii*) cash flow projections for the next 12 months; (*iii*) accounts receivable agings for the past 24 months; and (*iv*) a schedule of all salaries and other compensation paid to officers, shareholders, directors, or relatives during the past three years.
7. Generilou would maintain a full complement of insurance on all of its properties and provide a binder for coverage to the creditors' committee.
8. The creditors' committee would be notified of any new lawsuits brought against the company.
9. Generilou would develop a written business plan with respect to its ongoing operations.

10. Generilou would provide a preference analysis as regards any payments made by the company to (*i*) its trade suppliers during the 90 days preceding the general meeting of creditors and (*ii*) any insiders during the preceding 12 months.
11. Generilou's representatives and the creditors' committee would meet again (possibly via telephone conference call) in four weeks to review the data requested above and determine what courses of action should be taken.

Generilou's unusually large creditors' committee was made up of 12 individuals, 8 of whom were the aforementioned credit executives of the oil brokers and major oil companies. The other members were mostly vendors of services. This was not the most friendly or tolerant group of creditors that Generilou could have had. When you're facing the prospect that you won't be receiving any payments on your antecedent debt for an indefinite period *and* you know the debtor won't be doing any business with you in the intervening period (recall that Generilou was now phased out of refining crude oil), it is difficult to retain your objectivity. It would take a while for these creditors to cool off. They waited impatiently for the data being collected by the management and advisers of Generilou.

To the surprise of some of the skeptics on the creditors' committee, the information package was assembled and sent to HACM's adjustment bureau manager within the allotted two weeks. He made copies of the materials and forwarded them to the members of the creditors' committee. These folks then had two weeks to review the material prior to the next meeting with Generilou's negotiating team.

Generilou's representatives and the creditors' committee held a telephone conference call, as scheduled, four weeks after the first meeting of creditors. This was to be the day when the creditors were to get a small measure of, in a sense, revenge. Committee members were *not* happy to find that while Generilou was rapidly slipping into a financial quagmire, Ruston and Reese continued to pay themselves more than $200,000 per annum, each!

The chairperson of the creditors' committee began the meeting with the following demand: if the owners of Generilou were to retain cooperation from the creditors, they would immediately have to cut their compensation in half. If not, there was no point in going any further. Generilou's special insolvency counsel knew from experience that the bankruptcy court would probably agree that a sizable reduction in pay would be appropriate in the circumstances. He advised his clients to accept this impediment to going forward.

The creditors clearly did not think Ruston and Reese were suffering enough in their personal finances. With little resistance, they gave in to this demand. Although most people can get along fairly well on $100,000 a year, Ruston and Reese actually would have trouble making do. They had acquired a taste for the good life, including expensive homes with substantial mortgages. There was the distinct possibility that they could lose their homes to foreclosure. Did the creditors care? Not likely.

The creditors' committee, satisfied that Generilou had not made any material preference payments, had no reason to force the company into a bankruptcy proceeding to seek recovery of payments. In reviewing the balance sheets for the past few years, one of the committee members noticed there once was over $2.6 million in bank debt. What had happened to the banking relationship? Ruston indicated that a major bank, headquartered in New Orleans, had lent money to Generilou on a formula tied to accounts receivable. All of the company's assets had been pledged to secure the loan.

As the company's losses mounted, revenues began to decline and assets to shrink. Generilou's troubles with its bank escalated when the company defaulted on several affirmative covenants under the credit and security agreement governing the loan. The bank used this opportunity to accelerate the loan payments. Generilou paid off its bank loan prior to the end of 1984, primarily by leaning on its trade creditors. In effect, the company's suppliers became its bankers. When all of the bank's funds had been returned, the credit officer in the loan workout department, where the account had been transferred, suggested it would be a good idea for Generilou to take its business elsewhere. Within a few weeks, a new depository-only banking relationship was established with a local bank.

This was one of those rare occasions when a beleaguered debtor went before a group of creditors and did not state that all of the company's assets were pledged to secure the loan of a senior creditor. This was to become an important bargaining chip as the negotiations plodded forward. After six months, Generilou's representatives and the creditors' committee hammered out a reorganization plan acceptable to a substantial majority of the company's creditors—both in dollar amount of claims and the percent of claimants. HACM performed as the secretary of the creditors' committee and forwarded a copy of the bulletin shown in Exhibit 7–1 to all interested parties.

EXHIBIT 7–1
Bulletin Regarding Plan to Repay Unsecured Creditors' Claims

In the matter of

Generilou Oil Recycling Co., Inc.)	Bulletin No. 8
711 Bengal Way)	
Lake Charles, Louisiana 70699)	
————————————————)	

To the Creditors:

After four months of negotiations, we are pleased to report that settlement documents have been finalized by the owners, management, and representatives of Generilou (the Debtor) and your Creditors' Committee. Enclosed are the Debtor's Plan of Reorganization, Disclosure Statement, and a Ballot. We encourage you to carefully review the attached documents so that you will be fully informed as to the background of this case and the details of the proposed plan to satisfy all of the Debtor's outstanding obligations to unsecured creditors. Once you have read these data, please exercise your right to vote on the Debtor's proposal by completing the appropriate ballot and returning it in the enclosed envelope.

The Plan provides for the satisfaction of all claims of the Debtor's unsecured creditors that arose prior to March 27, 1985. Funding for the payment of the claims under the Plan will be provided from the net cash flows generated from the operation of the business. The Plan provides that allowed claims of unsecured creditors will be divided into two categories. The first category (Class 2 in the Plan) is for creditors with claims of $200 or less, or claims that are reduced to $200. These claims will be paid in full no later than 60 days after the implementation of the Plan.

The second category of claims of unsecured creditors (Class 3 in the Plan) is for those with amounts owing in excess of $200, excepting those who elect to be included in the first group. Class 3 claims are expected to be paid in full. However, given the Debtor's current financial condition, payment can only be accomplished over an extended period of time. Class 3 claims will

EXHIBIT 7–1 (concluded)

be paid from a special fund set up and administered by the Houston Association of Credit Management. The Debtor will make quarterly deposits into the fund, in accordance with the formula set forth in the Plan. Unsecured creditors may also benefit if the Debtor succeeds in collecting some of the claims it has against other businesses that have filed bankruptcy.

During the first year following the effective date of the Plan, the Debtor will not be required to make any deposits to fund the Plan. This payment deferral period is intended to allow the Debtor to augment the working capital it needs to facilitate the development and sale of products from its recycling technology. This continued delay in payments to Class 3 creditors was not viewed as very attractive by the Creditors' Committee. However, during the negotiations that led to this Plan, the Creditors' Committee evaluated other alternatives, including the liquidation of the Debtor. It was decided that, if the business ceased operating and its assets were converted to cash, unsecured creditors would receive less than 5 percent of the total amount owed. Given such a minuscule dividend, it was concluded that more could be expected from the Debtor's rehabilitation.

The debtor's management has projected sales of $18 million and net income of $400,000 in the next 12 months. Over the ensuing five years, revenues and profits are both projected to grow at a compound rate of approximately 30 percent per annum. Based upon these projections (presented more fully in the accompanying Disclosure Statement), the Debtor's management believes that "net cash flow" as defined in the Plan will be sufficient to pay all claims over a period of eight years. While the period is quite lengthy, the Plan appears to be the most viable one that can be effectuated. During the period that the Class 3 claims remain unpaid, the Creditors' Committee will continue to closely monitor the operations of the Debtor.

It is very important that creditors understand that the attached Ballot contains a Chapter 11 clause, which, in the event that the Debtor files a petition under the applicable provisions of the Bankruptcy code, shall be deemed to be a consent to any reorganization plan filed by the Debtor in the bankruptcy proceedings; provided, that the terms are not materially different from those set forth in the Plan. Your vote is extremely important. Attached hereto is a Ballot printed on brightly colored paper for your ease in recognition. Please return this Ballot as soon as you are able. If the Debtor is not successful in obtaining the consent of 85 percent of the unsecured creditors the Plan will not be implemented. We look forward to receipt of your affirmative response.

Very truly yours,

Manager
Adjustment Bureau

enclosures

The overwhelming majority of Generilou's creditors did respond affirmatively to the company's request that the reorganization plan be approved as presented. There really wasn't much of an alternative. Unfortunately, some dissident creditors would not go along with the program. They held about 10 percent in number of the total claims and 15 percent in dollar amount. They would accept nothing less than a liquidation of the business. Out-of-court turnaround plans cannot bind creditors who are unwilling to cooperate. They can still exercise their legal rights to pursue payments. Since Generilou had virtually no secured creditors, judgment liens could be effectively used by dissident creditors.

The solution to this problem was for Generilou to file what is sometimes called a "dip 11"—a quick filing of a preapproved Chapter 11 petition and a request for a speedy confirmation by the court. This is also known as a "cramdown" because it compels a minority faction to accept what is acknowledged by the majority to be fair and equitable treatment. Since the Disclosure Statement and Plan of Reorganization were already found acceptable to the legally required majority of creditors, the bankruptcy judge's job was virtually completed. Remaining to be determined was that full and adequate disclosure was made to allow creditors to make a well-informed decision. With the expert guidance of the attorney specializing in insolvency law, Generilou was able to meet all of the requirements set out in the Bankruptcy Code.[1]

---

[1] Comprehensive examples of a disclosure statement and a plan of reorganization are set forth in *Revitalizing Your Business,* another book written by the author.

CHAPTER 8

VOLUNTARILY ENTERING A LIQUIDATING CHAPTER 11, PERMITTING A SECURED CREDITOR TO FORECLOSE ON COLLATERAL, AND SUBSEQUENTLY REPURCHASING THE ASSETS

> The worst bankrupt in the world is the man who has lost his enthusiasm. Let a man lose everything else in the world but his enthusiasm and he will come through again to success.
>
> *H. W. Arnold*

There are many, many instances when even the most talented, dedicated, and hard-working business owners and managers cannot revitalize and then reorganize a company that has fallen on financial hard times. Frequently, despite clear evidence that a viable core business may exist, the conditions are simply not right to allow the interested parties to effectuate a workable plan to repay all creditors. Sometimes even the banks get caught with inadequate collateral to get their loans repaid in full. What happens in hopelessly insolvent cases such as these is the subject of this chapter. A recapitalization strategy will be presented that shows how the repurchase of specific assets formed the basis of a new enterprise with many of the same characteristics of the former business.

Generiel Hoist Rental Corporation (Generiel) and Generi-lift Construction Equipment Company, Inc. (Generilift), are our models for this refinancing technique. Generiel is a relatively young and now prospering corporation formed in 1984 for the sole and specific purpose of acquiring certain equipment and other assets previously owned by Generilift. The latter company had been established in 1964 and, until it ran into insoluble business troubles in 1982 and 1983, allowed its owners to earn a very comfortable living. Generiel and Generilift have two very important things in common. Roger Barnett was the founder and CEO of both companies. And the original business purpose for each was renting hoists for lifting personnel and material in the construction of high-rise buildings throughout southern California.

During its first 17 years in business, Generilift was a steady, if unspectacular, performer. The company was quite adept at riding the ups and downs of the business cycles that affected the construction industry in southern California. Barnett was able to expand and contract his business so well, in fact, that only once in Generilift's pre-1982 history had it experienced negative operating cash flow, and that was in 1975, a period of severe economic hardship for commercial and industrial builders as well as for the businesses dependent on them. Even then, the company's deficit cash flow was less than $100,000, and Generilift was able to cover the shortfall by temporarily leaning on and stretching out its trade payables.

On the strength of Generilift's excellent level of service, the consistently dependable operating performance of the company's equipment, and his own active involvement in trade association activities, Roger Barnett emerged as one of the most respected leaders in the construction industry. As the decade of the 1980s dawned, Generilift was in its best financial condition ever. Besides having a strong, relatively liquid balance sheet, the company had signed rental contracts in hand for virtually every one of its fleet of 30 construction elevators. The following 12 months were likely to produce more than $2 million in rental income and result in pretax profits of approximately $400,000. Little wonder Barnett was excited about Generilift's business prospects.

With the immediate future well under control, Barnett was able to direct his attention to long-range planning issues. Despite the very strong business climate of the moment, his long years of experience in the market indicated that the likelihood of a recession was growing more certain. Perhaps, he thought, this was the time to finally diversify into business activities not dependent on the southern California construction industry. With very little effort on his part, Barnett was introduced to what seemed at the time a fantastic business opportunity. One of the largest engineering and construction companies in the world asked Generilift to design and manufacture a hoist to carry men and material to the top of deep-well drilling rig platforms—almost the height of a five-story building.

A prototype was designed and manufactured by Generilift. After a period of rigorous testing was completed, a firm order for four more special-purpose hoists was placed. Over a 15-month period, from late 1980 to early 1982, all five hoists were delivered and put into operation in locations as far away as Kuwait. The international construction company readily acknowledged that the new hoists' adaptability, safety, and technology were much better than competing systems. Although Generilift's hoists were slightly more expensive than alternative means for lifting oil field workers and their specialized tools, Barnett received assurance that his company's hoists were the preferred product. Follow on business was almost a sure thing.

Barnett was so confident that Generilift's push into manufacturing was a good idea that he went out and *personally bought* a new building to house the operation. Generilift leased the property from Barnett at the same cost he was incurring to pay off the mortgages that he assumed to make the purchase. The facility was more than five times as large as Generilift's old run-down plant. Generilift's noncapitalizable costs of the move, which was completed in the spring of 1982, totaled $90,000. It was definitely a very attractive place to work. All Generilift employees derived a sense of pride in being associated with a company on the move. But, the new facility was also a heavy burden on cash flow.

Although Generilift had spent about $125,000 more than it had received in payment for the five drilling rig hoists (the company recognized the cost overrun at the completion of the contract in early 1982), Roger Barnett thought that sum was a small price to pay to become the supplier of an additional 150 hoists. He reasoned that the engineering and other uncovered costs would quickly be amortized as the production line began to hum. He was also confident that the average cost of a hoist would fall quickly as the production team moved down the learning curve. Other things being equal, Barnett's rationale would have been correct. Unfortunately, this business activity never quite made it past the starting gate. The oil glut that developed put an indefinite hold on orders as energy-related construction projects around the world ground to a screeching halt.

Most business owners and managers would probably have gotten depressed when the prospective buyer of another 150 hoists decided to suspend (and ultimately cancel) the follow-on order, which would have produced about $5.5 million in revenues for Generilift over a three-year period. Roger Barnett was naturally disappointed; but, being the strong-willed person he is, he did not let it get the better of him. He quickly set about to find another opportunity to make hoists. Through a series of phone calls to his broad network of friends and business associates, Barnett made contact with an ex-naval officer. The former military man was aware of, and for a small fee would share with Generilift, an opportunity that appeared on the surface to be even more attractive than the stalled drilling rig project.

The U.S. Navy was seeking bids from prospective manufacturers of hoists capable of lifting as much as 4,000 pounds of personnel and/or material in connection with dry dock ship overhaul work. Generilift's chief engineer and vice president of manufacturing expressed their opinions to Barnett that the company should have no problems handling this business. With the drilling-rig–related project on hold, it made a lot of sense to try and keep the production team together. The company was already experienced in making hoists with a 6,000-pound lift capacity, and it was building a prototype of a hoist with a payload of 7,500 pounds—the largest lift capacity in the market. Besides, Generilift needed to start producing revenues to spread some of the costs of operating the new building.

With the former Navy commander's expertise to guide them through the maze of applicable government regulations, Generilift was successful in bidding for, and winning, a contract to build four hoist prototypes. There was a great deal of initial excitement at Generilift because it seemed quite possible that the company might receive additional orders worth as much as $7.8 million. The advantages of becoming a virtual sole-source supplier for a major branch of the military were enormous. Of course, every business opportunity is accompanied by potential pitfalls. Fate, it seemed, was not on Generilift's side in this business venture either, as problems surfaced almost immediately. Over the strong objections of Generilift's engineer, the Navy's technical staff insisted that a number of changes had to be made in the design and specifications of the hoists. This basically meant that a cookie-cutter approach using existing Generilift engineering drawings would not be acceptable.

Generilift reluctantly complied with the uncompensated change orders because management was confident that over the long haul the company would be able to demonstrate the soundness of its approach and then persuade the Navy to reimburse it for the initial cost overruns. That assumption proved wrong. The Navy was to become Generilift's most intractable customer ever. This was not Generilift's first experience in dealing with a bureaucracy—the company interacted routinely with building inspectors, OSHA inspectors, and the like. It was, however, Generilifts first, and last, contract with the Navy. The strains in the business relationship only worsened as the initial phase drew to a close toward the end of 1982. The bottom-line result was that Generilift lost $165,000 on the Navy project. Barnett was not at all unhappy to say good riddance to this troublesome foray into manufacturing hoists.

As it always seems to happen with companies that get into financial trouble, Generilift's problems were getting worse on all fronts. The research and development costs (which had to be expensed as incurred) for the new hoist with the 7,500-pound lift capacity exceeded $215,000, and the company had still not worked all of the bugs out. Although a working prototype was in its testing phase, problems came up with the new dual-drive electronic logic and the onboard diagnostic panel. These features represented significant advances in the state of the art for hoists. The delay caused by the technical problems combined with the recession-induced softening in the demand for all types of construction-related equipment resulted in the expected orders for the new hoist not coming through. As tough-minded and confident as he was, Roger Barnett was beginning to have serious doubts about his ability to get through these diversification moves.

The coup de grace for Generilift was the 1982 recession. Roger Barnett knew that a downturn for the southern California construction industry was as inevitable as the sunrise. And when Generilift's customers have problems, so does Generilift. How right he was! In the span of just eight months, Generilift's equipment utilization rate dropped from 90 percent to 50 percent. Hoist rental fees were also hit, decreasing by an average of 20 percent. The ever-resourceful Barnett didn't cave in even with these added storm clouds. With the excess inventory of motors, gear boxes, plating, and other standard and interchangeable parts ordered in anticipation of the follow-on orders for drilling rig and dry dock hoists, Generilift undertook a major modernization program of its rental fleet. The cost of this program was eventually determined to be $255,000. Ironically, this decision turned out to be one of Barnett's best, forming the basis for the creation of Generiel. But more on that later.

Where, you might ask, did the money come from to finance the company's unsuccessful excursions into manufacturing? From Generilift's bank and suppliers, of course. But, you might respond, creditors such as those rarely, if ever, provide funding for risky ventures. That's true. It wasn't Barnett's intention to use working capital funds for investment purposes; that's just the way it turned out. Believe it or not, Roger Barnett's diversification plan for Generilift was predicated on raising outside capital. And this wasn't simply one of Barnett's whims, either. He spent a hundred-plus hours working with a respected regional investment banking firm to assist in the preparation of a prospectus for the purpose of raising $2.2 million in convertible subordinated debentures. The completed document explained how Generilift would pursue various opportunities, including those already in progress. Barnett was encouraged to believe that the securities could be privately placed with a small group of sophisticated investors.

Generilift's established good credit history and collateral package alone were probably sufficient to enable Barnett to obtain a mid- to upper-six-figure credit facility for his company. The investment banking firm's prestige and connections in southern California financial circles put Barnett in contact with a regional vice president of an independent bank who, in concert with a vice president-credit, had loan approval authority up to $1 million. It didn't take long for a new credit arrangement of that magnitude to be put together. The bank did seem to take the proper precautions—security interest in all of Generilift's assets, Barnett's personal guarantee, etc. In early 1982, a luncheon with senior bank officials got the new relationship off to a great start. All that remained was for Generilift to perform.

For a while, the company did appear to be making great strides in its efforts to build a viable manufacturing operation. The bubble burst, however, in the fall of 1982. The investment banker suggested that Generilift's chances of obtaining the desired amount of capital from private investors would be greatly enhanced if the company's financial statements were audited by a Big Eight accounting firm rather than by the small CPA firm that had provided tax and accounting services for the past 10 years. In fact, Generilift had never had an audit performed. Review-level statements were the extent of previous outside examination. Barnett met with representatives of three of the prominent national CPAs. The idea of spending $35,000 for a full-blown audit was not attractive to Barnett, but Generilift's need for additional cash was already causing problems with trade creditors who were not being paid in accordance with agreed terms. In late November, he selected one of them, and the process of discovering how bad things really were began.

By the time the outside auditors finished their work in the latter part of February 1983, it was determined that Generilift had *lost* almost $800,000 during 1982. The noncapitalizable and unrecovered costs of the diversification projects, the move to new facilities, and the fleet modernization program totaled $850,000. Worse yet, the company appeared to be continuing to lose money, and it had an accumulated *deficit* net worth of approximately $500,000. A senior partner and the manager of the engagement from the CPA firm met with Roger Barnett to explain the probable consequences.

When the bank credit officers studied Generilift's year-end audited financial statements, they would probably come unglued because the interim operating statement through the first 10 months of the year indicated the company was marginally profitable. It just didn't compute. How could a business lose $800,000 in two months? The previous accounting was, to be kind, shoddy. One problem was that inventory had not been properly relieved when the contracts with the Navy and the construction company were completed. Another was that many of the hoist modernization costs should, in accordance with generally accepted accounting principles, have actually been recorded as repair and maintenance charges, not capital expenditures.

Although the bank knew Generilift's cash flow was tight, it was not aware of how bad things had actually gotten. One thing was sure: Generilift was in technical default on numerous terms and conditions of its loan and security agreement. The bank was almost certain to exercise its right to accelerate payment of the full amount of the outstanding loan balance. Without the bank's forbearance and/or the investment banker obtaining alternative or supplemental sources of financing, the company's ability to continue as a going concern was highly questionable. The accounting firm said that releasing the audited financial statements could very well precipitate crises with creditors from which the company might not recover. Barnett knew he would have to bear the brunt of the problem sooner or later, so he decided to confront the situation head on.

Barnett met with his account officer at the bank in late March to discuss the situation. That bank official took the bad news rather stoically, Barnett thought to himself on his way back to Generilift. Less than a week later, however, he was invited (*summoned* is perhaps a better word) to another meeting—this time with the head of the bank's loan workout department. At the second meeting, Barnett was asked point-blank (by the man in the proverbial black hat) to explain how the company was going to begin repaying the bank's loan. Generilift's CEO was at a loss. He was still in somewhat of a mental fog from the CPA's devastating financial report, and he hadn't given a great deal of thought to the subject of debt repayment. The loan workout officer tried to be sympathetic (although you couldn't prove that to Barnett), but he had a job to do. Barnett was strongly encouraged to retain a financial consultant to assist in the preparation of a detailed cash flow forecast. He was given three names from which to choose and two weeks to produce the financial data requested.

Barnett quickly got his act together and retained a financial adviser. It took a while for Barnett and the consultant to piece together the worst-case scenario, but they finished the cash flow forecast in the required time frame. Given the recession and current less-than-50-percent equipment utilization rate, the cash flow forecast indicated that Generilift could do little more than keep the doors open. The company could barely pay interest under the present conditions. Principal payments would need to be temporarily suspended.

At Barnett's request, the financial adviser called the company's contact officer at the bank to set up a meeting to discuss the new projections. The account officer asked that the data be messengered to the bank in advance, so that the loan workout department could review the numbers in detail before the meeting. In a few days, the account officer called Barnett to set up another meeting. It would be a good idea, the banker suggested, if Barnett brought Generilift's attorney or, better still, an insolvency lawyer with him. Barnett was, as you can well imagine, startled. Why would he need to bring his lawyer? And what the hell is an insolvency lawyer? The bank must be up to something. Barnett was right.

The meeting was opened by the bank's attorney. The bank's loan workout department did not believe the company could recover from the financial setbacks it had recently experienced, and, accordingly, the bank wanted Generilift to immediately file a liquidating Chapter 11. The scenario presented in the cash flow forecast was unacceptable. The bank could not, or would not, wait for an indefinite period to be repaid. Furthermore, Generilift was clearly losing money every day it remained open, and there was the very real chance that the company's unsecured creditors would file an involuntary Chapter 7 anyway. And if the suppliers didn't get to the company first, the Internal Revenue Service would because it was owed $25,000 in payroll taxes withheld from employees but not paid.

Roger Barnett pleaded with the bank's representatives that if Generilift filed Chapter 11, it would never be able to reorganize. The business would slowly but surely wither away as the remainder of Generilift's rental contracts expired. Several of the company's customers' policies stated that no new contracts would be entered into with any supplier filing a bankruptcy petition. Barnett's reasoning fell on deaf ears. It was the bank's assessment that the maximum loan recovery would result through this strategy. It had a blanket security interest in all of Generilift's assets as well as Barnett's guarantee. The bank wanted Barnett to enter the liquidating Chapter 11 voluntarily, but it was prepared to force the issue by foreclosing on its collateral if it had to do so. Barnett acquiesced to the bank's "request." (At the suggestion of one of Barnett's good friends who had gone through financial problems himself, Generilift did pay off the obligation to the IRS before filing its bankruptcy petition. The owners and managers of a business cannot absolve themselves of the personal responsibility to pay these obligations.)

Over the next eight months, Barnett's dire prediction of Generilift's demise came to pass. Although there were signs that the construction industry was on the verge of a recovery, Generilift had great difficulty getting new business. Chapter 11 was starving the company to death. By January 1984, the company's equipment utilization rate had dropped to about 15 percent. The business was wilting away, and, as it did , the bank's deficiency grew. To get a more precise idea of the magnitude of the probable loan loss, the bank retained an equipment appraiser/auctioneer (whose opinion was very well respected by the loan workout department) to come in and place an under-the-hammer value on the fleet of hoists and miscellaneous other spare parts inventory, furniture, fixtures, and equipment. The value determined was an incredibly low $250,000. Given the nature of this special-purpose equipment, there were a very limited number of prospective buyers for the hoists. The bank's remaining loan was a little over $550,000. Thus, a charge-off of approximately $300,000 was likely.

Barnett felt very strongly that the assets (in particular, the hoists) were worth far in excess of the liquidation value placed on them by the auctioneer. He thought the hoists alone were worth $2 million, if not more. The higher valuation was true, however, only if the hoists were operated by persons as skilled in using them as Roger Barnett and his remaining skeleton crew. A rule of thumb is that assets like the hoists will liquidate for only about 10 to 20 percent of their replacement value. The solution to the puzzle was for Barnett to somehow retain control of the hoists. How could that be done? Simply and swiftly, if the proper inducement could be offered to the bank. Generilift's attorneys could arrange for the bank to obtain what is called "relief from the stay," which means that the bank could ask the bankruptcy court to allow it to foreclose on and dispose of its collateral. If Generilift consented to the proposal, there was a good chance it would be approved.

The deal was struck when Barnett agreed to repurchase the assets from the bank for $550,000 and give the bank a personal note for $50,000 secured by his residence. The small personal loan would be used for working capital in the new company. A new corporation, Generiel, was formed to acquire the assets. Since Roger Barnett had no cash resources, the transaction would need to be financed with new loans from the bank. The loan workout group would have preferred being cashed-out, but the idea of liquidating the hoists for less than half of what Barnett offered and writing off the balance of the loan was not very attractive.

The possibility of recovering the remaining principal on the bank's loan had definite appeal to the loan workout department. Although it would probably take five years for Generiel to repay the noninterest-bearing $550,000 note, the discounted value of the payment stream was still appreciably higher than the current liquidation value. In addition, if building activity were actually on the rise, the value of the equipment would be rising. Thus, if Generiel defaulted on its loan payments a year later, the collateral might be worth more than now. Despite all of the other rationalizations put forth to facilitate the recapitalization of Roger Barnett's business, *the* deciding factor was that Barnett had demonstrated very convincingly to the bank that he was one hell of an exceptional manager when his undivided attention was riveted on the hoist business. The bank really did want to help Generiel emerge from this unpleasant experience as a successful business.

When the transaction was completed, Generiel's beginning balance sheet had $600,000 in assets, $550,000 in liabilities, and $50,000 in net worth. Since Generiel, unlike Generilift, was not in Chapter 11, it was able to actively solicit business from all of Generilift's former customers. Roger Barnett had made quite a few friends in the construction industry, and he quickly found out that business was again readily available. Within a year, he had gotten the equipment utilization rate back to 60 percent of capacity. In less than two years, the rate hit 85 percent. Generiel kept a very lean organizational structure, and its cash flow was positive from day one. Barnett felt he had been pushed to the brink and survived. He was so chastened by this brush with business failure that he developed a preoccupation with attaining and keeping a very liquid financial position.

Whatever became of the approximately $600,000 in unsecured debts that were the obligations of Generilift when it filed its bankruptcy petition? The claims weren't dismissed or forgiven, but after the bank was permitted by the bankruptcy court to foreclose on all of its collateral, Generilift had no assets remaining with which to pay any other creditors. Eventually, the case was converted to a no-asset Chapter 7 bankruptcy—a subject covered in greater detail in Chapter 11 of this book.

In the years that followed, many of the unsecured creditors who received nothing from Generilift resumed doing business with Generiel. At first, all business was done on a COD basis. Barnett did not have a financial responsibility to any of the former unsecured creditors, but he felt a moral obligation to make some amount of restitution to those creditors. Generiel now has open lines of credit with a sizable number of Generilift's old suppliers. As a matter of policy, though, the company pays all of its bills within 15 days of their receipt.

CHAPTER 9

ARRANGING A PRIVATE SALE OF ASSETS TO AN "ANGEL" AT A COMMERCIALLY REASONABLE PRICE

All problems become smaller if you don't dodge them, but confront them. Touch a thistle timidly, and it pricks you; grasp it boldly, and its spines crumble.

William S. Halsey

A very large number of businesses in this country have come ever so close to achieving the ambitious hopes and dreams of their owners only to be brought crashing down to reality as their financial, marketing, and operational support systems disintegrated. Quite often, the managers of these financially troubled businesses couldn't see, or didn't heed, the early warning signs. I call this problem entrepreneurial hyperopia—a perceptual flaw of business owners and managers who do have a reasonably good vision of the distant future but are unable to recognize and avoid the hurdles that must be cleared in the present to accomplish their long-range objectives.

Some of the best examples of entrepreneurial hyperopia are to be found among high-tech enterprises. It remains undeniably true that the future is very bright for many thousands of high-tech businesses. The rapid proliferation of extraordinarily useful, technology-driven products and services over the past decade is a clear testimonial to that fact. The personal computer and the word processing program that enabled me to write this book are the best examples I can possibly imagine. Just a few short years ago I was literally incapable of preparing a simple business letter because my typing skills were so poor. Now I am able to run my own business with very little need for administrative support.

Of course, growing numbers of influential political and economic leaders believe high-tech businesses hold the key to restoring America to its preeminence as *the* world economic power. This type of environment attracts *billions* of dollars of risk capital. It is also a medium that breeds intense competition, fleeting interests, and rapidly advancing changes in the state of the art. If a business remains on the right side of the power curve, the experience for the owners and managers is exhilarating. If it fades to the wrong side, the apprehension of reality for all concerned is enervating. In high-tech businesses, the deterioration process can be incredibly swift.

It is very frustrating to see a business with many of the elements needed to be successful but without quite enough of them to enable it to survive a severe financial setback. Occasionally the core of a business can be salvaged and later reappear as a successfully reorganized business. This chapter involves such a company—Generitech Peripheral Equipment Corporation (Generitech). This Denver-based company was established in 1977 by Maxwell Templeton and Donald Segesi to engineer, manufacture, and market various types of printers. Both men were engineers with advanced degrees. They also had extensive experience with large mainframe computer makers.

Right from the start, Generitech's emphasis was on in-house engineering and quality. Over a period of seven years, the business developed an impressive line of printers for use in data recording, labeling, personal computers, and hardcopy imaging of data displayed on computer monitors (videoprinters). In the early years of Generitech's growth, most of its printers were used in scientific and medical applications. With the explosive growth of the personal computer market in the early 1980s, more than half of the company's business was derived from the sale of dot matrix and letter-quality printers. Revenues and after tax profits rose steadily over the years, reaching a peak of $8.7 million and $280,000, respectively, in 1984.

Other things being equal, this company should have continued evolving into a very good business with solid market niches. Like many others, Generitech did experience some financial problems when the shakeout occurred in the PC market in 1985. The company had to write off more than $150,000 in uncollectible accounts receivable from stores specializing in PCs and related products. Those retailers had gotten into financial straits themselves, and, although they had sold Generitech's products, they were not able to make payments to Generitech. Legal efforts to collect the receivables proved unproductive. Some of Generitech's customers actually had to file bankruptcy.

Generitech's accounts-receivable–based credit facility at its bank went into "overloan" status, meaning the company's borrowings had exceeded the agreed limit of an 80 percent advance rate against eligible A/R. Generitech managed to overcome this liquidity squeeze by restructuring its credit arrangement. A temporary 25 percent advance was made against Generitech's qualified inventory. The bank would have preferred not making an inventory loan to this high-tech company, but Max Templeton and Don Segesi were very persuasive in their efforts at convincing the account officer that the loan would be repaid in short order. The company did have a core of other products that had continued to do well. Management's good track record with the bank up to this point weighed heavily in their favor. The request for more money from the bank was approved.

Generitech probably could have weathered the relatively minor financial setback involving uncollectible accounts receivable. The circumstance that contributed most directly to Generitech's irreversible financial difficulties was a fluke, not at all predictable. Although Templeton and Segesi could hardly be faulted for financial problems caused by the blunders of others, the resulting cash flow difficulties nevertheless proved disastrous for the owners of Generitech.

Subsequent to the problems that arose with the company's entry into the PC market for printers, Templeton and Segesi made the strategic decision to once again concentrate Generitech's business activities in commercial, scientific, and medical applications. At a weekend planning meeting held in Aspen to get everyone's undivided attention, Generitech's owners, managers, and engineers concluded that the products with the greatest market potential were going to be ultra-high-resolution videoprinters. Such products reproduce images from highly refined CAD/CAM/CAE graphic display screens with such clarity that they almost have the appearance of a photograph.

Generitech was already involved in engineering and manufacturing videoprinters in the mid-range of quality and sophistication, but its products could not exactly be described as state of the art. With constant attention to changes in the market, Generitech engineers were quite adept at keeping the company's existing products competitive. However, while Generitech's leap from its current line of videoprinters into the ultra-high-resolution market was technically feasible, it would require quite a bit of human and financial resources to accomplish.

The uncertainty and risk of entering a relatively uncrowded but extremely quality-conscious market segment did not escape Templeton and Segesi. These men were not prone to making sudden, speculative decisions that might result in financial problems down the road. They thought long and hard about how much it would cost to get Generitech's proposed new products to market. After multiple iterations on their own PCs, the bottom line of their detailed project budget was that about $1.9 million would be required to do the job right.

Templeton and Segesi realized that neither they nor their company had the financial wherewithal to undertake the project without some outside financial assistance. Without even asking, they quickly concluded that their bank would not be interested. Venture capital financing would undoubtedly be needed if the program was to have any chance of succeeding. At the time, quite a bit of risk capital seemed available to companies like Generitech. They decided to prepare a detailed investment memorandum (the contents of which were very similar to the one outlined in Exhibit 2–1) and then go searching for funding.

It didn't take too long for Generitech to find an interested venture capitalist, and practically right in the company's own back yard. A highly regarded financing whiz who had previously worked for well-established venture capital organizations based in New York and California decided to strike out on his own in early 1984. His national reputation allowed him to quickly succeed in obtaining commitments from several large pension funds, insurance companies, and banks to establish a $30 million venture fund, which he would manage. With a fondness for skiing and hiking, he elected to set up shop in a suburb of Denver so that he could actively pursue his professional and personal interests on a year-round basis.

Over a 12-month period, he actively sought out, and found, a number of high-tech companies similar to Generitech. After a relatively quick due-diligence analysis, the venture capitalist decided he liked the company's prospects enough to fund the entire $1.9 million project for 45 percent of Generitech's common stock. The form of the investment was a convertible subordinated debenture. Since, at the time, Generitech's net worth was only $400,000, the proposal seemed very attractive. Templeton and Segesi agreed to the offer from the venture capitalist. Within a few short weeks the necessary documents were executed.

The only problem was that funding for the high-resolution videoprinter development project was not made in a lump sum. The initial advance was $475,000—more than enough to get started but not nearly enough to finish if, for some reason, the funding balance did not materialize. As fate would have it, the venture capital fund *itself* ran into severe problems. More than half of the investments made in other high-tech companies turned sour. Those troubled businesses rapidly absorbed nearly all of the venture fund's resources. When it came time for Generitech's next drawdown, no funds were immediately available. The venture capitalist assured Templeton and Segesi that additional funding would be forthcoming from the fund's backers, but it would take a little time.

Unfortunately, the project could not be frozen in time. Salaries for the project engineers had to be paid, some specialized materials had to be purchased, and so forth. To tide the company over until the next installment arrived from the venture fund, Generitech went to its bank to obtain still another temporary advance. The bank's senior credit administrators were again very reluctant to provide additional financing; but, after a lengthy meeting with the account officer, Generitech's management, *and* direct communication with (and assurances from) the venture capitalist, the bank agreed to increase its inventory advance rate to 50 percent. This bridge loan, however, was expected to be repaid from the next venture funding. The bank, which already had a blanket security interest in all of Generitech's assets, required Templeton and Segesi to personally guarantee the restructured loan and secure its repayment with second mortgages on their homes.

The weeks dragged on, and still there was no money forthcoming from the venture fund. Unbeknownst to Generitech's management, the venture capitalist had used up all of the institutional investors' funds on those previously noted problems. The investors became so upset with the unsatisfactory performance of the portfolio companies that they decided to cut off further funding and oust the fund's manager. The new man was charged with the responsibility for stopping the bleeding in the portfolio and, if possible, recovering money. This obviously would have adverse ramifications for Generitech, but several weeks passed before Templeton and Segesi discovered the magnitude of the problem. It turned out that $475,000 was all Generitech would ever get from the venture fund. The project was only a little more than half finished.

After four months, the bank's credit officers became deeply concerned that the venture financing had not materialized. The bank began to apply verbal pressure on Generitech's management to reduce the inventory loan. But, since funding was still needed to finance the new videoprinter, management kept stalling. When the company went into default under the credit and security agreement, the bank took a more decisive step. It began to systematically take back its funds by applying 10 percent of all Generitech collections to the loan balance.

The cash flow pressures resulting from reducing the bank loan and financing development of the videoprinter intensified, and Generitech did the only thing left to do. It stretched out its payables as far as it could. The company's biggest and most important vendor became extremely upset about the situation and insisted that the only way it would continue to do business with Generitech was if the company granted it a junior security interest in all of its assets. Generitech simply had to have certain parts from this crucially important supplier, so Templeton and Segesi gave in to the demand.

To compound matters further, the new portfolio manager finally got around to meeting with Templeton and Segesi. He informed them that the fund had exhausted all of its resources and, not only would no additional funds be advanced, but the fund wanted to develop a program to see its *loan* repaid. When Templeton said he thought the money obtained from the fund was an investment (as in equity), the venture capitalist suggested that if they checked the documentation they would see it was actually debt. After Generitech's owners explained the company's financial troubles, it was agreed that if the fund would defer principal reductions for a year, the company would grant the fund a security interest in its assets. At the time, the new fund manager thought this was an acceptable arrangement. It was only later discovered that being in third position behind the bank and the vendor was tantamount to remaining an unsecured creditor.

Generitech's cash flow problems soon became so severe that the company could no longer finance its operations. The bank, in effect, was assisting the company in an orderly liquidation. When a few of the unsecured creditors decided to seek legal remedies to collect past-due invoices, Templeton and Segesi sought legal advice. One of the ideas suggested was the filing of a Chapter 11 petition. This idea was dismissed when the owners realized that such a maneuver might ultimately result in loss of their residences if the strategy did not work out and the bank was left with a deficiency against its claims. Another alternative discussed was using NACM's Denver affiliate. This idea, too, was thought impractical because Generitech was fading so quickly that it couldn't survive a three- to six-month turnaround period.

What Generitech needed was an "angel" to come to its rescue. And quickly. It so happened that one of the company's largest customers was already keenly interested in Generitech's high-resolution videoprinter. The prospective angel's chief engineer understood exactly what Generitech's engineers were doing and, more important, how close they were to completing the prototype. The long-term value of Generitech rested on the completion of the new videoprinter project. Without it, Generitech was not an attractive investment opportunity for the angel.

It didn't take long for the imaginative minds of the owners and managers of the two businesses and their legal and accounting representatives to devise a plan to recapitalize Generitech. At first, the angel's attorneys tried to get the largest unsecured and less-than-fully-secured creditors to accept token compromise payments. When these efforts proved unsuccessful, a straight asset buy was recommended by the company's attorneys and subsequently proposed by the angel to Generitech's bank. The bank was not at all reluctant to discuss the idea. Although some risks were associated with employing this strategy for getting the bank's loan repaid, the loan agreement clearly stated that one of the bank's rights was to foreclose on and then sell the assets securing its loan.

Summarized in Exhibits 9–1 through 9–5 is the procedure used to effectuate the sale of all Generitech assets to the angel. The entire process took less than a month. When the transaction was completed, Generitech was a corporation with no assets but plenty of remaining liabilities. It wouldn't do unpaid creditors any good, however, to file or continue lawsuits against Generitech if there were no assets. Even if judgments were obtained, no assets would be left to satisfy them.

Given the complex legal nuances associated with this recapitalization technique, consultation with highly competent attorneys is strongly recommended for both debtors and secured creditors. Much of the carefully worded correspondence was prepared under watchful eye of legal counsel.

EXHIBIT 9–1
Letter from an "Angel" to a Lending Institution Proposing the Purchase of Generitech's Assets at a Private Sale

Dear Lending Institution Vice President:

Computer Peripheral Equipment Mfg. Co., Inc., through a new subsidiary to be formed in the State of Colorado (herein below referred to as Subsidiary), is interested in purchasing all of the assets of Generitech Peripheral Equipment Corporation (Generitech). As you are acutely aware, Generitech is having extreme financial difficulties in meeting its current obligations to creditors,

EXHIBIT 9–1 (continued)

and it is in default under a number of the terms and conditions of the Credit and Security Agreement between Generitech and your lending institution, dated April 23, 1985.

We have previously discussed with your lending institution a plan by which our company would satisfy all of the debts of Generitech by payment of various sums to the various classes of creditors, in full and complete satisfaction of their respective claims. Regrettably, this program has not proven viable. Certain secured and unsecured creditors have rejected the offers that were made to enable Generitech to discharge its obligations to them.

Given these recent developments as well as the fact that Generitech's business is rapidly losing momentum, we would like to propose a new plan in which all of the assets of Generitech are purchased by our Subsidiary from your lending institution, pursuant to a private sale arranged in accordance with the terms and conditions of the Credit and Security Agreement noted above, and in compliance with the requirements of all applicable commercial codes and laws. It is our understanding that a secured creditor is allowed to dispose of its collateral in this fashion so long as the private sale is conducted in what a prudent and responsible individual would consider a commercially reasonable manner.

More specifically, we request that your lending institution consider the following proposal. Upon the transfer of all of Generitech's assets to our Subsidiary, we, Computer Peripheral Equipment Mfg. Co., Inc., will, through the Subsidiary:

(i) Pay, in cash, all sums due and owing to your lending institution, including all of the costs incurred in connection with the obtaining and disposing of the Collateral.

(ii) And additionally, deliver a promissory note in the sum of $200,000, which note should constitute excess proceeds from the sale of the Collateral and, therefore, should be transferred to the secured creditor with the next-highest-priority claim. We believe that the amount being offered is higher than could be realized from the liquidation of the assets by your lending institution or one of its agents.

In consideration for this payment by our Subsidiary, your lending institution would thereupon execute a Bill of Sale to our Subsidiary, transferring all of the rights, title, and interest in, and to, the Collateral as defined in the Credit and Security Agreement.

This proposal is the result of lengthy discussions with the executive officers of Generitech, who have expressed their strong belief that a purchase of all of the assets of Generitech by our Subsidiary from your institution, via a private sale, would be in the best interests of the business, its shareholders, and other interested parties. Your prompt evaluation of this proposal would be greatly appreciated. The rate of deterioration of Generitech's business has accelerated to the point that the value of the Collateral could dissipate quickly.

This letter should not be construed as a formal offer to acquire the Collateral in question. Rather, it is intended as an outline for further discussions between and among all of the interested parties to the proposed transaction. If the terms of this letter are acceptable to your lending institution, our respective legal counselors can meet to develop it into a definitive agreement.

EXHIBIT 9–1 (*concluded*)

Thank you for your consideration. I look forward to hearing from you at your earliest convenience.

Yours truly,

John M. Oberheim
Chief Executive Officer
Computer Peripheral
Equipment Mfg. Co., Inc.

EXHIBIT 9–2
Reply from Lending Institution to "Angel's" Proposal to Acquire Generitech's Assets at a Private Sale

---

Dear Mr. Oberheim:

Receipt is hereby acknowledged of your letter of last week regarding the account relationship of Generitech Peripheral Equipment Corporation (Generitech) and this lending institution. As a result of various events of default under the Credit and Security Agreement between Generitech and this lending institution, dated April 23, 1985, it is our intention to accelerate the outstanding indebtedness of Generitech and to exercise the rights of a secured creditor to sell the assets of Generitech at a private sale.

We are favorably impressed with your proposal. Provided that we can comply with all of the requirements of the above-referenced Credit and Security Agreement, as well as all applicable laws and commercial codes, this lending institution is prepared to go forward with your company in a private sale of Generitech's assets. Please be aware, however, that we must consider any and all offers for such property. It is our express intention to send notices to all of the shareholders of Generitech and to all of its creditors concerning this matter. In the event your offer is the highest available, and it is deemed by our legal counsel to be commercially reasonable, we would be pleased to enter into a definitive agreement with your company.

If you have any questions, please do not hesitate to call.

Sincerely,

William M. Stang
General Counsel
Lending Institution

EXHIBIT 9–3
Notice by Lending Institution to Generitech's Shareholders Regarding Its Intention to Enter into a Private Sale of the Assets which Secure Its Loan

To: The Shareholders of Generitech Peripheral Equipment Corporation

Notice is hereby given that the properties described herein below, which constitute the Collateral as defined in that certain Credit and Security Agreement (Agreement) dated as of April 23, 1985, and executed by Generitech Peripheral Equipment Corporation (Debtor), and the undersigned lending institution (Secured Party), will, as a consequence of the Debtor's default under said Agreement, be sold by the Secured Party at a private sale to be held on, or after, the 10th business day following the date of this notice.

The assets to be sold are described generally as follows:

(*i*) All goods of the Debtor including, but not limited to, machinery, equipment, furniture, furnishings, fixtures, tools, and supplies of every kind and description.
(*ii*) All inventory of the Debtor including, without limitation, raw materials, work in process, finished goods, merchandise, parts, and supplies of every kind and description.
(*iii*) All accounts and notes receivable, contract rights, money, customer lists, business records, trademarks, patents, patent applications, good will, and other general intangibles of every kind and description.
(*iv*) All documents, instruments, and chattel paper.

Dated_____

Lending Institution
By:_____
Its: Senior Vice President

EXHIBIT 9–4
Notice by Lending Institution to General Creditors of Its Intention to Enter into a Private Sale of the Assets which Secure Its Loan to Generitech

To: The General Creditors of Generitech Peripheral Equipment Corporation

Please be advised that Generitech is in multiple default of the terms and conditions of its Credit and Security Agreement (Agreement), dated as of April 23, 1985, with this lending institution. Upon the execution of the Agreement and the funding of the loan, this lending institution was granted a first-priority lien on all of the assets of Generitech. The lien was contemporaneously perfected with the filing of the required documentation with the appropriate governmental agency. A copy of the duly filed and recorded UCC-1 document is attached hereto for your information and review.

EXHIBIT 9–4 (concluded)

Generitech has been unable to remedy the events of default under the Agreement. Accordingly, this lending institution intends to exercise its right as a secured creditor to foreclose upon and then sell the collateral by means of a private sale. We have received a proposal from Computer Peripheral Equipment Mfg. Co., Inc., to buy all of the assets of Generitech, in bulk, at such a private sale. We invite any other parties interested in making a competing bid for this collateral, to contact us immediately.

In our opinion, as well as in the view of the shareholders, managers, and advisers of Generitech, such a private sale to the proposed purchaser would be a sale in a commercially reasonable manner and would, in actuality, represent an excess over the fair market value of the assets being sold. We are confident that the price being offered is, under the circumstances, the best price that could be obtained for the collateral.

The proceeds of the private sale will result in the full payment of all of the outstanding principal and interest owing to this lending institution. There is, unfortunately, the likelihood that there will be little or no proceeds available, after the repayment in full of our debt, to satisfy the claims of other creditors, excepting the secured creditor with the next-highest-priority claim.

It is our intention to conclude this private sale on, or after, the 10th business day following the date of this notice. Enclosed herewith, please find a copy of the notice given to the shareholders of Generitech indicating our intention to conduct a private sale of the assets collateralizing the indebtedness owing to this lending institution. If you or your legal advisers would like to obtain any additional information, please make contact at your earliest convenience.

Dated_____

Lending Institution
By:_____
Its: Senior Vice President

EXHIBIT 9–5
Letter from the Chief Executive Officer of the Newly Formed
Subsidiary of Computer Peripheral Equipment Mfg. Co., Inc. to
Generitech's General Creditors

To: The General Creditors of Generitech Peripheral Equipment Corporation

A few weeks ago, you were notified of Computer Peripheral Equipment Mfg. Co., Inc.'s intention to purchase all of the assets of Generitech from the company's secured lending institution at a private sale. The lending institution had acquired the assets by exercising its rights as a secured creditor through a peaceful foreclosure. We wish to inform you that the transaction has now been completed. I am the new chief executive officer of a subsidiary company formed to carry on the business that was formerly conducted by Generitech.

EXHIBIT 9–5 (concluded)

Among the assets that we acquired from Generitech's former lending institution were the name of the company and the trademark, "Generitech." It is our intention to conduct business under the dba (fictitious business name) of Generitech as well as to use the trademark "Generitech" on future products that are developed and sold by our company. It is our desire to continue to work with as many of the former suppliers of Generitech as possible. I realize that it will take time to reestablish credit lines with you, but as we get to know one another better, I think you will find the "new Generitech" to be deserving of credit.

We are attempting to maintain a continuity of operations by retaining as many key employees as possible. In that regard, we have entered into employment contracts with Maxwell Templeton and Donald Segesi. They will serve as vice presidents of research and operations, respectively, of the new company. We have also assumed the lease on the property that has been Generitech's principal place of business for the past seven years. We hope that the transition will be as smooth as possible for everyone concerned.

If you have any questions regarding the new company, please do not hesitate to call Max, Don, or me.

Sincerely,

Michael R. Kensington
Chief Executive Officer
CPEM-Colorado Corporation
dba Generitech

The good news about this recapitalization strategy is that it can be done quickly and privately. The bad news is that an asset sale leaves the former stockholders of the troubled business with little or no ownership of the new company. In Generitech's case, Templeton and Segesi were retained as employees, but their ownership interests in CPEM-Colorado Corporation were reduced from 100 percent to 10 percent. However, when one considers the alternative, this was still the best choice. The former owners of deeply troubled Generitech faced the prospect of losing their company as well as their jobs and maybe their homes. In the final analysis, it is far preferable to own a minority interest in an enterprise with good-to-excellent potential than to own all of a business in danger of failure.

CHAPTER 10

MAKING A GENERAL ASSIGNMENT FOR THE BENEFIT OF CREDITORS AND STARTING OVER

Big shots are only little shots who keep on shooting.

Christopher Morley

A "general assignment for the benefit of creditors" is a rather large mouthful of words that mean the shareholders of a troubled business have decided the time has come to give up fighting with those to whom they are financially indebted. In essence, the owners are throwing in the towel. This *strictly voluntary* procedure is the state court equivalent of a business filing for a Chapter 7 liquidation under the U.S. Bankruptcy Code. It can be used in many cases with a great deal of effectiveness.

The case of Genericom Advertising International (Genericom) is a good illustration. Genericom was created in Los Angeles by Gena Blume in 1977. She had the requisite credentials to become a fast-tracking executive at a major New York-headquartered ad agency that had a West Coast office. Although her career was advancing quickly in comparison to others in the firm, the pace wasn't rapid enough nor, in her estimation, was her level of remuneration. After months of planning, she announced that she was leaving to start her own agency.

Much to the surprise of no one, Blume quickly made Genericom into a terrific success. Billings of just under $1 million in the first full year of operations quickly jumped to $12 million by the end of the seventh year. One extremely good bit of luck helped fuel the company's development. In the mid-1980s, Genericom was able to take advantage of a temporary glut of quality office space in L.A. The company leased an entire floor of a high-rise building and received six months' free rent. Although the landlord had wanted Blume to personally guarantee the lease payments, in the final analysis that point did not become a deal breaker, and the owner of Genericom escaped what was to become an important issue.

With attractive, tastefully decorated, new offices, Genericom was able to project an image of a company with everything going for it. Its enhanced stature vis-à-vis the other advertising boutiques was an important facet of Genericom's own marketing program. For a while, the plan worked well. Genericom was able to add new clients much more easily than it had previously. The bulk of the agency's business was derived from several fast-growing companies engaged in high tech, consumer electronics, health and beauty products, entertainment, office management, sportswear, travel, and exercise equipment.

As a result of Genericom's growth, it became one very exciting and creative place to work. Blume was able to recruit some of the best young talent in the area. The ads that were created won many awards, which greatly pleased and motivated the staff. More important, the clients were happy because they were achieving higher sales volume for their products and services. The agency's management had done a good job of convincing their clients that Genericom was responsible, at least in part, for the successful ad campaigns.

Most important, from her own perspective Blume was gratified because she had accomplished what she set out to do and was pulling down a salary in the low six figures. She was being considered as the subject of a major magazine article about successful women executives. In short, Blume was living very well (but not extravagantly). She made a number of good investments, including a beautiful home in one of the most desirable parts of southern California. She was beginning to believe it would never end. But, of course, things did change for the worse.

Genericom began 1986 on an apparently sound financial footing. Unfortunately, as the weeks went by it became clear that three of the company's major accounts were having financial troubles, which, in turn, caused cash flow problems for Genericom. To ease its liquidity crunch, the company went on a new business development blitz. In an effort to generate new sources of billings, Genericom relaxed its credit and collection policies even further. The strategy exacerbated the situation and resulted in more erosion in the customer base.

Up to this point, Genericom had never needed to borrow. Its flow of funds was such that the company paid its creditors with moneys it received from clients. Genericom had never had a major account go south on it. This was a new experience. Blume and her VP–Finance went to a number of banks and commercial finance companies to seek a short-term working capital loan. When the lenders saw the concentration of business with a small number of clients and the amount of accounts receivable in the past-due category, they quickly turned down the request for credit.

Genericom's inability to pay its bills as they came due was reaching critical proportions. The agency owed more than $2.5 million to scores of radio and television stations, magazines, newspapers, photographers, lithographers, graphic artists, typographers, and assorted other media or production companies involved in the dissemination of advertising. The pressures on the accounting department became unbearable, and Blume was called on to personally respond to the calls from increasingly hostile credit managers. She could do little but explain that Genericom's problems were the result of its customers not paying their bills.

On the advice of her legal and financial advisers, Blume decided to write a letter to all of Genericom's creditors in the hope that it would explain and defuse the situation. It was a carefully worded, comprehensive description of the misfortunes that had befallen Genericom. (See Exhibit 4–1 for a more detailed example of this strategy.) The letter's closing paragraph stated that the company hoped it would be permitted to successfully reorganize without having to file a bankruptcy proceeding. To that end, it was critical that creditors not bring legal actions against Genericom to collect what were, admittedly, valid claims against the company.

The letter did buy Genericom a few weeks' time, but the

situation did not improve. In fact, it deteriorated further. The company's largest account filed Chapter 11. Genericom was owed approximately $800,000 at the time, and there was little likelihood it would see any of the money at any time in the near future—if ever. A few of Genericom's more sophisticated, or less patient, creditors decided to try and collect payment through legal means. Blume knew instinctively that this was not an equitable way to deal with creditors.

The next step was to either file a bankruptcy petition or attempt an out-of-court solution through the NACM affiliate in Los Angeles. The latter course was selected because it seemed to have a fair chance of working and did not preclude Genericom from filing Chapter 11 if things did not succeed. The meeting was quickly arranged. Within 10 days, Blume and her advisers were given the opportunity to present the situation in person to all interested creditors. At that first meeting, it was mentioned that a number of creditors had chosen to take independent action to collect the funds due them.

Genericom did not want to let the more aggressive creditors have an unfair advantage, but it also did not want to file bankruptcy it if could be avoided. It found a solution. The company agreed to grant a security interest in its assets to *all* of its unsecured creditors. Thus, even if one or more of its creditors filed suit, obtained a judgment, was granted a writ of attachment, and attempted to have the marshall's office execute on the court order, a previously existing secured third party could protect the assets of the business. An example of such a simple, yet powerful, document is shown in Exhibit 10–1.

EXHIBIT 10–1
Security Agreement with Previously Unsecured Creditors

For good and valuable consideration, receipt of which is hereby acknowledged, Genericom Advertising International, a California corporation having its mailing address and principal place of business in the City of Los Angeles, hereby grants to Credit Managers Association of California, as Trustee for the present unsecured creditors of Genericom, a security interest in all of Genericom's tangible and intangible personal property, both presently owned and hereafter acquired, including, but not limited to, the following:

1. All present and future accounts, contract rights, chattel paper, security agreements, insurance proceeds, supplies, money, documents, notes,

EXHIBIT 10–1 (continued)

drafts, investments, instruments, and general intangibles (including all present and future causes in action, goodwill, trademarks, trade names, customer lists, purchase orders, deposit accounts, and tax refunds).
2. All present and hereafter acquired furniture, furnishings, fixtures, motor vehicles, and all equipment, accessories, replacements, additions, and improvements to any of the foregoing.
3. All of the proceeds of the property listed in paragraphs (1) and (2) above.
4. All present and future books and records pertaining to any of the fore-going.

All of the foregoing is hereinafter referred to as Collateral. In the event Genericom fails to pay the indebtedness secured by this instrument upon demand and reasonable notice by Secured Party; or if Genericom suffers an attachment, levy, or seizure of the Collateral; or causes or suffers the commencement of proceedings by or against Genericom under any bankruptcy law; or makes a general assignment for the benefit of creditors; or causes or permits the appointment of a receiver or trustee for Genericom; or suffers a tax lien notice by any taxing authority; or ceases normal business operations; or fails to keep Collateral properly insured; or fails to pay taxes when due; or sustains a loss through theft, damage, sale, or removal of Collateral; then, the Secured Party shall have the right to take possession of the Collateral and the Secured Party shall have the rights and remedies of secured parties under the California Commercial Code and applicable California law.

This Security Agreement is made and shall be construed under, pursuant, and according to the laws of the State of California. Waiver of any default or provision shall not be, or be deemed to be, a waiver of any subsequent or other default or provision.

All rights of Secured Party under and pursuant to the terms and provisions of this instrument and applicable law shall inure to the benefit of Secured Party's successors and assigns, and all obligations and duties of Genericom hereunder shall be binding upon Genericom's successors and assigns.

If any portion of this Security Agreement violates or is prohibited by any code, regulation, statute, or law of any territory, state, country, or other political subdivision in which it is intended to be operative, any such portion shall be deemed to be null, void, and of no force or effect whatsoever, provided however, that the remaining portions of this instrument shall be deemed to be in full force and effect.

Dated: _____

Genericom Advertising International,
    a California corporation

By: _____
    Gena M. Blume
    Chief Executive Officer

EXHIBIT 10–1 (concluded)

ACCEPTANCE

The security interests created in the foregoing Security Agreement are hereby accepted at Los Angeles, California.

Dated: _____

Credit Managers Association of
  California, as Trustee for
  the Present Unsecured Creditors of
  Genericom Advertising International

By: _____
  Manager, Adjustment Bureau

The security agreement that Blume executed on behalf of Genericom proved very effective. The company's attorneys were able to discuss the merits of this legal procedure with the attorneys representing the most intractable creditors. Nearly everyone went along. Those creditors electing not to cooperate discovered, in due course, that they were unable to overcome this barrier. The legal maneuver worked primarily because all creditors remained in their same relative positions.

Creditors become extremely uneasy when they don't know what is going on. They assume the managers of troubled businesses are going to—deliberately or unwittingly—make preference payments to selected creditors. This happens often enough that it is probably safe to assume it will occur. In the absence of any certain knowledge, some credit managers become very aggressive in their pursuit of claims. If they succeed in obtaining what amounts to a preference payment, either through pressure or a lawsuit, one of the few means available to recover the payments is to file bankruptcy.

With the creditors temporarily at bay, Genericom's management and outside advisers tried everything they could to stop the flow of red ink. They cut salaries; they eliminated positions; they did everything possible to turn the business around.

It wasn't working. The insolvable problems were key employee defections and the loss of major accounts, which are not unusual occurrences in service businesses like advertising.

Creative and talented individuals apparently want the freedom to make their ideas come to life. The imposition of tight financial controls does not fit in well with their value systems. It was too easy for some of Genericom's best people to pack up and move on. Despite strong loyalty to Blume, they felt that outsiders were now largely responsible for what was happening to the agency.

Client relationships suffered badly as well. Advertising campaigns sometimes take months to develop. Genericom's clients obviously did not want to begin any significant new projects until the company could demonstrate that its financial affairs were in order. Some of Genericom's competitors were only too happy to report any and all of the company's problems. It was only a matter of time until talk of Genericom's imminent demise became a self-fulfilling prophecy.

Blume spent a very long weekend agonizing over what to do. Her most trusted friends and advisers suggested she give it up. She could, quite literally, hand the keys over to someone else and walk away. She decided to write a memorandum (shown in Exhibit 10–2) to Genericom's creditors before throwing in the towel.

EXHIBIT 10–2
Memorandum to Creditors prior to Making a General Assignment

To: The Creditors of Genericom Advertising International

From: Gena M. Blume
      Chief Executive Officer

Subj.: Decision to discontinue operations and make a General Assignment for the Benefit of Creditors

As you are no doubt well aware by now, during the past few months Genericom has been operating under intense financial pressures. I have spoken to many of you personally in an effort to explain that my company's difficulties were, for the most part, brought about because some of Genericom's clients became ensnarled in problems of their own. I wish that I could report to you that the situation is getting better; regrettably, things have continued to worsen.

EXHIBIT 10–2 (*continued*)

Earlier this year, independent negotiations with certain creditors proved unsuccessful, resulting in legal actions on their part to recover claims against Genericom. When it became apparent that there was no viable alternative, we sought to protect the equitable interests of all creditors by convening a creditors' meeting under the auspices of the Credit Managers Association of California (CMAC). You were notified subsequent to that meeting, that a creditors' committee was formed to represent your interests while a repayment plan was negotiated.

During the ensuing few weeks, working through CMAC, your creditors' committee and Genericom developed an effective means of deflecting legal efforts by individual creditors attempting to enforce their rights. More specifically, a security agreement was entered into granting a blanket collateral interest in all of Genericom's assets to CMAC, as Trustee for all the unsecured creditors of the company. Previously, Genericom had no secured creditors, except for a few equipment lessors whose claims were very minor. This measure did enable us to achieve the stability needed to begin negotiating a plan to reorganize Genericom.

A subsequent event has occurred, however, which makes Genericom's attempt at business revitalization all but impossible. It was mentioned in a previous communication from CMAC to you that retaining the company's principal client relationships was the cornerstone of Genericom's turnaround effort. Those six accounts represented nearly 50 percent of the company's projected cash receipts for the next 12 months. We were recently informed by three of our most important clients that under the circumstances they were compelled to allow other agencies to bid for their business.

In the past, Genericom responded to setbacks such as this by putting on an intensive marketing campaign to develop new account relationships. In the company's already weak financial condition, it makes little sense to pursue that strategy. We could prolong the agony by filing a Chapter 11 petition, but that action would merely result in the further dissipation of Genericom's assets. Accordingly, I have instructed the company's attorneys to prepare the required documentation for me to make an assignment of Genericom's assets to CMAC for the benefit of creditors. CMAC will be in contact with you as to the significance of this decision.

I have reluctantly given in to the recommendations of my legal and business advisers because I honestly believe that the time has come to turn the liquidation of the business affairs of the company over to CMAC. The immediate future is not very promising. When CMAC converts all of Genericom's liquid assets to cash and sells the very nominal amount of furniture, fixtures, and equipment the company owns, the net cash proceeds will probably be under $250,000. With total liabilities exceeding $2.5 million, the near-term recovery will be tiny.

I emphasize near term because I think that some portion of Genericom's sizable portfolio of delinquent accounts receivable will ultimately be paid. Unfortunately, the payments will not arrive in time to salvage the company. Our continued efforts to collect on these old invoices would not be cost effective. CMAC and its collection department is organized to follow each of the accounts to their logical conclusion.

EXHIBIT 10-2 (concluded)

In closing, I want to express my sincere appreciation to those of you who supported me for so long while I tried every means at my disposal to turn Genericom around. I know some of you are bitterly disappointed that my efforts to pay you proved to be unsuccessful. I am deeply embarrassed and humiliated by the outcome of recent events, but there are not other alternatives left to pursue.

Respectfully submitted,

Gena M. Blume

Blume's decision to write one last, highly personalized communication to Genericom's creditors was critically important if she wanted to immediately get back into advertising. Most people can readily accept the fact that financial reversals are a part of doing business—no one is immune to making mistakes in judgment. On the flip side, most people have no sympathy, or respect, for those who decide to hang onto their jobs and paychecks in the face of incontrovertible evidence that a business turnaround is impossible to accomplish.

Filing Chapter 11 would probably have given Genericom a few more months to live, but it would very likely also have ended up ruining Blume's credibility in the close-knit advertising community. By doing the right thing, as most disinterested observers would agree, she was able to focus attention on the fact that Genericom was about to expire—but in a dignified, perhaps even noble, manner.

Make no mistake, a general assignment for the benefit of creditors is a sure, swift means of terminating an enterprise. In fact, it becomes an estate. Assignees are not in the rehabilitation business. They exist to do one thing: get as much as possible, as fast as practicable, for the creditors they represent. Exhibit 10-3 shows Genericom's general assignment.

EXHIBIT 10–3
General Assignment

THIS ASSIGNMENT, Made this __24th__ day of __June__, 19__87__

BY _____ Genericom Advertising International

of (address) _____ 15300 Wilshire Boulevard, Suite 1400

_____ Los Angeles, California 90025

in the City of __Los Angeles__, County of __Los Angeles__
State of California, party of the first part, hereinafter referred to as Assignor, to Credit Managers Association of California, a California corporation, of Los Angeles, California, party of the second part, hereinafter referred to as Assignee.

WITNESSETH: That said Assignor, for and in consideration of the covenants and agreements to be performed by the party of the second part, as hereinafter contained, and of the sum of One Dollar ($1.00) to Assignor in hand paid by said Assignee, receipt whereof is hereby acknowledged, does by these presents grant, bargain, sell, assign, convey, and transfer unto said Assignee, its successors, and assigns, in trust, for the benefit of Assignor's creditors generally, all of the property of the Assignor of every kind and nature and wheresoever situated, both real and personal, and any interest or equity therein not exempt from execution, including, but not limited to, all that certain stock of merchandise, store furniture and fixtures, book accounts, books, bills receivable, cash on hand, cash in bank, deposits, patents, copyrights, trademarks and trade names, insurance policies, choses in action that are legally assignable, together with the proceeds of any existing nonassignable choses in action that may hereafter be recovered or received by the Assignor.

This assignment specifically includes and covers all claims for refund or abatement of all excess taxes heretofore or hereafter assessed against or collected from the Assignor by the U.S. Treasury Department, and the Assignor agrees to sign and execute power of attorney or all other documents as required to enable said Assignee to file and prosecute, compromise, and/or settle, all such claims before the Bureau of Internal Revenue, U.S. Treasury Department, and agrees to endorse any tax refund checks relating to the prior operations of said Assignor's business and to deliver such checks to the Assignee.

Leases and leasehold interests in real estate are not included in this assignment. However, if the Assignee shall determine that the same may be assigned and also that the same has a realizable value for creditors, then the Assignor agrees that upon written demand of the Assignee, he will assign and transfer said lease or leasehold interest to said Assignee, or his nominee (subject to the written consent of the landlord if required under the lease), for administration under the terms of this general assignment.

Contracts and/or agreements between Assignor and any Labor Union, or Trade Associations, are excepted from and not included in this assignment.

The Assignor authorizes the forwarding of his or its mail by the U.S. Postal Department as directed by the Assignee.

Said Assignee is to receive the said property, conduct the said business, should it deem it proper, and is hereby irrevocably authorized at any time after the execution hereof to sell, lease, or otherwise dispose of said property upon such time and terms as it may see fit. Said Assignee shall use and apply the net proceeds arising from the conducting of said business and from the sale, or lease, or other disposition of said property as follows:

FIRST: To deduct therefrom (or to reimburse itself with respect to) all sums which said Assignee may at its option pay for the discharge of any lien on any of said property and any

EXHIBIT 10–3 (*continued*)

indebtedness which under the law is entitled to priority of payment, and all expenses, including a reasonable fee (as hereinafter defined) to the Assignee, and to its attorney, and to the attorney for the Assignor; and, in those instances where a creditors' committee has been selected at any meeting of the creditors of the Assignor (without regard to the actual amount or number of creditors present at such creditors' meeting) then a reasonable fee shall be paid to the attorney appointed by said Creditors' Committee in an amount fixed by the said Creditors' Committee and said Assignee.

SECOND: The balance of the proceeds then remaining shall be paid to the creditors of the Assignor, pro rata, according to the several indebtedness due to them from the Assignor.

With respect to the fees of the Assignee referred to in the aforementioned paragraph FIRST hereinabove, Assignor hereby expressly and irrevocably agrees as follows: That the term "a reasonable fee to Assignee," as used herein, is defined as, and includes the following: (a) An administration fee computed on the basis of the total moneys handled in connection with this Assignment and for the assembly, inventorying, collection, and liquidation of the assets assigned, in accordance with the following schedule, as specified in the Rules and Regulations of the Adjustment Bureau of Credit Managers Association of California, to wit: the greater of a minimum fee of $2,500, or on the first $5,000 of such total moneys, a fee of 9 percent shall apply; plus, and on the second $5,000 of such total moneys, a fee of 8 percent shall apply; plus, and on all moneys in excess of $10,000 a fee of 5 percent shall apply; (there shall be excluded from the foregoing, however, moneys received or disbursed in connection with and incidental to any actual continuing operation of the business assigned, as distinguished from moneys received in connection with the collection and liquidation of the assets assigned.) In addition to the foregoing, nonmembers of the Credit Managers Association of California, a California corporation, shall pay and the Assignee shall retain an additional fee of 6 percent of the amount of the dividends payable hereunder to each such nonmember creditor of the Assignor. In addition to the foregoing, the Assignee shall be entitled to the further sum equal to an opening charge of $20 to cover the expense of opening the records of this assignment case, a docket charge of $2 for each claim filed by any creditor in this assignment case, and reimbursement of first-class postage for each Bulletin issued to each creditor in this assignment case. In addition to all the foregoing fees and charges, the Assignor expressly agrees that the Assignee shall be entitled to a further fee equal to any and all interest earned and received by the Credit Managers Association of California on any trust and other funds in its hands and arising from this assignment. The Assignor further agrees that any and all dividends not claimed by creditors of the Assignor herein shall, after a period of two years from the date of the closing of the administration of this assignment, be retained by the Assignee as additional fees earned by it for its services hereunder; plus (b) when applicable in the opinion of the Board of Directors of Assignee, an additional reasonable sum for special, unusual, or extraordinary services actually performed by Assignee in connection with the operation, management, preservation, or administration of the property of the Assignment; and, in this connection the Board of Directors of the Assignee corporation, or the president of the Assignee corporation, is hereby given the right and discretion to determine the nature and extent of such special, unusual, or extraordinary services, and the amount of additional fees in connection therewith.

The total of all of said fees shall be paid from the property assigned, and from all of the proceeds thereof, and from any interest, income and increments, and any additions thereto.

Assignee hereunder shall be liable only in his or its official capacity for reasonable care and diligence in administering the estate created by this assignment.

Assignor as to all existing creditors extends the statute of limitations upon their respective claims for a period of one year from the date hereof.

Said Assignee is also authorized and empowered to appoint such agents, field representatives, and/or attorneys, and/or accountants as it may deem necessary, and such

EXHIBIT 10–3 (*continued*)

agents and/or field representatives shall have full power and authority to open bank accounts in the name of the Assignee or its nominees or agents and to deposit assigned assets or the proceeds thereof in such bank accounts and to draw checks thereon and with the further power and authority to do such other acts and to execute such papers and documents in connection with this assignment as said Assignee may consider necessary or advisable.

IN WITNESS WHEREOF, the said parties have hereunto set their hands the day and year first above written.

Genericom Advertising International

Gena M. Blume

Chief Executive Officer

and President

CREDIT MANAGERS ASSOCIATION OF

CALIFORNIA   a California corporation

By: _____
          Manager, Adjustment Bureau

Consent of Directors to Hold Meeting

_____ Los Angeles _____ , California
_____ June 24, _____ , 19 87

We, the undersigned, being all of the directors of the __Genericom Advertising__ __International__ _____ a corporation, organized under the laws of the State of __California__ , assembled this day at the office of the Corporation at __Los Angeles__ , California, do hereby consent that a meeting of said directors be held at this time and place for the transaction of such business as may come before the meeting, and waive any notice of said meeting.

_____ Gena M. Blume _____   _____

_____   _____

_____   _____

Minutes of the Meeting

_____ Los Angeles _____ , California _____ June 24 _____ , 19 87

At a meeting of the directors of the __Genericom Advertising International__ , a corporation, held at the office of the Company at __15300 Wilshire Boulevard__ , __Suite 1400__ California, at __10:30__ o'clock __A.__ M., the following directors were present:

EXHIBIT 10–3 (*continued*)

Gena M. Blume

Absent:

The President announced that the purpose of the meeting was to consider the financial condition of the company and the advisability of making a general assignment for the benefit of creditors.

On motion by __Gena M. Blume__ , seconded by _____Gena M. Blume_____ , the following resolution was adopted, to-wit:

BE IT RESOLVED:

That any two of the officers of this corporation be, and they are, hereby authorized and directed by the directors of this company, in meeting assembled, to make an assignment of all the assets of the corporation to Credit Managers Association of California, a California corporation, of Los Angeles, California, for the pro rata benefit of all creditors of this corporation, and that any two officers be, and they are, hereby authorized and directed to execute said assignment containing such provisions as may be agreed upon between them and said Credit Managers Association of California, a California corporation (Assignee) and they be also authorized and directed to execute and deliver to said Credit Managers Association of California, a California corporation (Assignee), such other deeds, assignments, and agreements as may be necessary to carry this resolution into effect.

BE IT RESOLVED FURTHER:

That said assignee for the benefit of creditors be, and it hereby is, authorized to execute and file and prosecute on behalf of this corporation all claims for refund or abatement of all excess taxes heretofore or hereafter assessed against or collected from this corporation and any one officer of this corporation be, and he is, hereby authorized and directed to make, execute, and deliver in favor of such person as may be designated by the assignee for the benefit of creditors, a power of attorney on the regular printed form thereof used by the United States Treasury Department so as to authorize said attorney-in-fact to process any tax claims for it on behalf of this corporation.

There being no further business to come before the directors, the meeting adjourned subject to the call of the President or Vice-President.

_____Gena M. Blume_____
Secretary

I, __Gena M. Blume__ Secretary of the _____Genericom_____
_____Advertising International_____ , a corporation,

do hereby certify that the foregoing is a true and correct copy of the minutes of the meeting of directors held in _15300 Wilshire Blvd., Suite 1400, L.A., CA 90025_ at the place and hour stated, and that the resolution contained in said minutes was adopted by the directors at said meeting, and the same has not been modified or rescinded.

EXHIBIT 10–3 (concluded)

Dated _____ June 24 _____ , 19<u>87</u>   _____ Gena M. Blume _____
                                                                    Secretary

CORPORATE
SEAL

Consent to Assignment by Stockholders

We, the undersigned, being owners and holders of __<u>100 percent</u>__ shares of stock, being more than 50 percent of the subscribed and issued stock of __Genericom Advertising International__, a corporation, do hereby give our consent to the within assignment and transfer of the property of said corporation.

Name	Shares Held
Gena M. Blume	100 percent
Chief Executive Officer	
and President	

The general assignment Blume consented to make on behalf of Genericom's creditors did close the book on that chapter of her life, but she quickly discovered there is life after debt. The substantial salary and many perquisites were gone. And the power and prestige that accompany the position of CEO had to be relinquished. But Blume still had all of the personal assets she had accumulated. These were not a part of the general assignment. Nor did they need to be disclosed. Unless the assignee discovered that Blume had done something illegal (which, of course, she hadn't), she would essentially be off the hook.

It didn't take long for Blume to sign on with another agency in town. She had made quite a few friends over the previous 10 years, and word on the street was that Blume had done a masterful job of making the best of a horrible situation. She was still a very talented advertising executive. The experience of Genericom was quickly erased from public view and consciousness. Having once tasted the sweetness of entrepreneurship, it was probably only a matter of time before she would build another successful advertising agency.

In many, perhaps most, cases of terminally ill businesses, the owners believe if they invest some of their personal resources, they will be able to turn the company around. This is usually a mistake of monumental proportions because those funds not only will have a negligible impact on the outcome of the severely damaged company but they could also be used as seed capital to finance another venture, including the establishment of the same type of business. In this instance, the best recapitalization strategy resulted in the closure of one company and the preservation of personal capital to facilitate creation of an entirely new one.

CHAPTER 11

FILING A VOLUNTARY CHAPTER 7 BANKRUPTCY PETITION AND STARTING OVER

Poverty is uncomfortable; but nine times out of ten the best thing that can happen to a young man [or woman] is to be tossed overboard and compelled to sink or swim.

James A. Garfield

Failure is probably the word most feared by owners and managers of small- and medium-sized businesses. And for good reason. The probability that a newly formed business establishment will fail is much greater than its probability of success. Something on the order of 80-plus percent of all new business formations end up as casualties in the war among competitors; more than half never reach their fourth birthday. Despite such a low success rate, in the entrepreneurial 80s, business creation is surging ahead. Clearly, most of the new business owners must believe they will be the roughly 1 in 5 or 10 that beat the odds.

Failure in the context of this book means losing nearly all of one's own financial resources as well as dissipating those of other investors and creditors with capital at risk in the business. Learning how to fail with grace and dignity is not an especially easy, or even welcome, concept. In truth, most American business owners and managers are prepared to go down with the ship in their efforts to keep a faltering business afloat. Sadly, most of them do, never to be seen as spirited entrepreneurs again. They typically find employment in similar lines of business—but as lieutenants, not captains, of industry.

The final days of a hopelessly insolvent business are usually filled with rancor and recriminations between the debtor and its creditors. On a worst-case basis, the hostilities are such that (as few as) three creditors who are owed a combined $5,000 join forces to put the business into an *involuntary* Chapter 7 bankruptcy proceeding. This means attempting to legally remove the present owners and managers and install a trustee, appointed by the bankruptcy court, to liquidate the business and distribute the proceeds in accordance with a well-defined set of legal priorities.

The usual response by the business's owners is to fight back by seeking to convert the case to a Chapter 11 debtor-in-possession status. In today's environment, the latter has an excellent chance of occurring. The outcome may not change—that is, the business fails—but the attitude of creditors toward the owners is probably damaged irreparably. Many creditors will perceive of these actions by the owners and managers as little more than a scheme to keep their incomes going for as long as possible.

There is, in the author's opinion, a better way to handle irreversibly injured enterprises. It is the business equivalent of euthanasia (mercy killing). Like that highly charged medical and moral issue, the willful decision to end the life of a business without exhausting every possible alternative (that is, spending every last dime permitted by the legal system) will not be readily embraced by all concerned. But there is a profound difference. Ending the life of a terminally ill business does not mean ending the lives of the owners. I am not in the least bit qualified to say whether or not there is life after death, but I can assure the reader there is life after debt. And sometimes it is better, certainly more serene.

This chapter's problem business deals with an enterprise that got into such a deep financial mess that it could not hope to recover. Its owners and managers could have stretched the period over which the business failed and thereby earned themselves a few more dollars. However, after a great deal of analysis and soul searching, they came to the right conclusion and took the right step—they filed a *voluntary* Chapter 7 bankruptcy petition after they had carefully developed and implemented a plan to wind down the operation. Even the most obstinate creditors begrudgingly admitted that the management of the business had performed in an extraordinarily professional manner. As a consequence, most of the employees and managers were quickly able to move on to other endeavors without being tainted with the label of failure. This is how it was done.

Generice Catalog Company, Incorporated (Generice), was founded by Brian Thatcher in a suburb of Cleveland in late 1984. Generice was a mail-order business that primarily sold consumer electronic products to the public through catalogs. Thatcher's entry into the catalog field was indirectly launched like many other small businesses—as a sideline. In 1980, while working full time in the marketing department of a large Ohio manufacturing company, he started selling specialty consumer items through space advertisements in controlled-circulation magazines. He was moderately successful in these early endeavors, supplementing his income by about $1,500 per month. His new business venture was literally an out-of-the-garage operation that he and his wife were able to manage during evenings and weekends.

In the recession of 1981–82, Thatcher was one of the hundreds of unfortunate souls victimized by a reduction in force by his employer. It seemed to him that 15 years of dedicated, loyal service were down the drain (except for the fully vested pension benefits he would begin receiving in 20 years, assuming the company made it that far and honored its commitments under the retirement plan). After a few months of searching unsuccessfully for another position as a marketing executive, it was only natural that Thatcher turned his attention to what was previously an avocation. In 1983, he introduced his first mail-order catalog to complement his space ads. It was only eight pages long, the photos were black and white, and he personally wrote all of the copy. (It was, he thought, enormously helpful to have had a lot of prior experience as a copywriter.) Thus was born Generice Catalog Company, Inc.

Thatcher then rented 100,000 names from a New York-based list broker, and he was off and running. The pull (or response) rate was unexpectedly strong. Nearly 2 percent of those receiving the catalog responded with an average order of about $85. Thatcher figured he netted about $12,000 from the initial mailing. He decided the time had come to devote all of his time, energies, and money into making the business grow. He expanded the mailings to four times a year. Pretty soon he had to move out of the garage and into a small warehouse. In no time, his small proprietorship was grossing close to $1 million a year. The formula seemed to be working splendidly. In early 1985, he made the commitment to concentrate entirely on catalogs and ended the space ad business.

Generice grew rapidly over the following 12 months. The catalog was expanded to 24 pages; four-color photos were used; some of the copywriting was farmed out; a relationship was established with one of the country's largest printing companies; and 300,000 names were rented from list brokers. On the surface, things were looking pretty good. Although Generice's growth quickly consumed all of Thatcher's personal capital, he was able to obtain sufficient amounts of trade credit to keep the engine running.

Acting on the good advice of his friendly banker, who noticed that Generice's financial ratios were getting out of balance, Thatcher began searching for additional capital. Although he was a virtual novice in the money-raising game, much to his surprise, within a few short weeks he found a venture capital firm keenly interested in his business. (As discussed in Chapter 2, the probability of finding funds serendipitously is very low, but it happens often enough that everyone simply has to try for it.)

Actually, the enthusiastic venture capitalist had studied this segment of the catalog market very carefully and had already decided there was a good opportunity to make money by investing in it. A half-dozen similar ventures had produced excellent results for their owners and other venture funds. The Generice catalog seemed the perfect blending of an idea whose time had come, a bright and aggressive owner, and professionally managed money. The venture firm contacted several other prospective venture capital investors, who also indicated a preliminary interest in participating in the financing, subject to the confirmation of certain financial and operating data. Thatcher hired a Big Eight accounting firm and a highly regarded law firm to facilitate matters.

While the venture capitalists and Generice's advisers were conducting their due diligence, Thatcher was moving quickly to line up more manufacturers, suppliers, and prospective customers. He attended virtually every consumer electronics trade show in the world that year. Based primarily on the *anticipation* of an infusion of new venture capital funds, suppliers financed the production and distribution of 4.8 million catalogs in three separate drops during the first six months of 1986. Manufacturers sent hundreds of thousands of dollars of merchandise to Generice. Virtually all of these transactions were based on open credit terms. It is rather remarkable that a business less than three years old could amass such large amounts of unsecured trade and vendor debt.

In late June 1986, four venture capital firms invested $2.4 million in Generice. The documentation for the transaction was about an inch-and-a-half thick. The affirmative and negative covenants were drawn very tightly. Among other things, Thatcher was expected to immediately begin a search for a new chief operating officer and a new chief financial officer to assist in managing the business. Unfortunately, Thatcher was so busy handling other matters that he did not have the time to locate and hire qualified executives for those positions. After two months, the board gave him specific instructions to retain a search firm to get the job done. Despite the board's insistence and his own good intentions, the management team was not assembled until late December 1986. By then, it was too late.

As it turns out, the injection of new capital had the effect of adding gasoline to an already out-of-control fire. Approximately 10 million beautifully produced, four-color catalogs, expanded to 64 pages, were delivered in three mailings during the second half of 1986. Scores of new importers as well as domestic manufacturers were clamoring to get their products into the Generice catalogs. And many new copywriters, photographers, list brokers, and other suppliers were eagerly bidding to do business with the company.

Not surprisingly, Generice's growth in revenues soared. Sales in 1986 came in at just over $14 million, a ninefold increase over 1985. As 1987 began, it appeared to Thatcher that Generice was well along the way to achieving his (and the venture capitalists') lofty goal of becoming a $100 million public company within five years. The situation could not have been much better in the view of Brian Thatcher. Sure there were problems, but with the new management team in place, the controls would soon be established and the next set of objectives could be pursued.

The new chief financial officer, however, was discovering some rather unnerving facts. Many of the (by then) more than 340 vendors who had provided products and services to Generice were making noises that they wanted to be paid. Some had actually gone to court to gain satisfaction for their claims. This didn't make sense for a company that seemed profitable and, only seven months before, had received funding that should have carried it for at least another year's growth. Although cash flow was tight, no one suspected that the problems were as bad as they actually were. In February, the new members of management persuaded the venture capitalists to ante up another $1.2 million while they and the outside CPAs sorted out the financial facts and figures.

The newly installed chief operating officer, who had more than 20 years' experience as a senior executive in the mail-order catalog business, set about to find out what the problems were. He quickly discovered that Generice's pull rate for 1986 was an abysmal 0.6 percent. An acceptable response rate would have been above 1.5 percent. The huge flood of orders obscured the fact that the people receiving Generice's catalogs were not buying very much of the products being offered.

He also found that catalog production costs alone were nearly $8 million, and mailing costs added another $1.5 million. No meaningful analysis was being performed to evaluate whether or not Generice's merchandising formula was working. It was simply assumed that the gross profit margin was high enough to cover the enormous selling, general, and administrative costs the company was incurring. Profit-per-item analysis was not being done very effectively because the analysts were not experienced and not properly supervised.

After a month or so of assessing the situation, the new chief operating officer concluded that the approach to merchandising was seriously flawed and that the current look of the catalog was not sufficiently attractive to interest prospective buyers of the company's products. Although there were other marketing problems, those two factors were primarily responsible for the low pull rate. If they were not modified—and soon—Generice would not be able to solve its problems. Under the best of circumstances, months are required to effectuate such changes because it takes time to redesign the catalog, shoot new photographs, prepare new copy, and select new mailing lists.

The accounting firm spent a great deal of time (and, as it would later turn out, absorbed sizable uncollectible fees) trying to put Generice's financial statements into shape. It was a very difficult assignment because the company's books and records were in a terrible state of disarray. This was not unusual for a business that did $14 million in revenues with an average ticket size of about $100, which translates to about 140,000 separate orders. That is a lot of information and paperwork to keep track of, and, although Generice did lease a very powerful computer system to handle the job, experienced personnel were not in place to manage the data processing function.

When the dust settled, the accounting firm could not give Generice a clean bill of health. The loss in 1986 was a whopping $4.9 million! Even with the infusion of $3.6 million in equity capital and subordinated debt, Generice was in grave financial shape. After several frustrating, partner-level meetings, the accounting firm decided that a qualified opinion would need to appear in any financial statement bearing its name. The following language was to be used:

> The accompanying financial statements have been prepared on a going-concern basis, which contemplates the realization of assets and the satisfaction of liabilities in the normal course of business. As shown in the accompanying financial statements, Generice has a retained deficit of $2.1 million at December 31, 1986, and its total liabilities exceed its total assets by $2.3 million. These factors, among others, indicate that the company may be unable to continue as a going concern. The financial statements do not include any adjustments relating to the recoverability and classification of assets or liabilities that might be necessary should Generice be unable to continue in existence. The company's continuation as a going concern is dependent upon its

ability to generate sufficient cash flow to meet its obligations on a timely basis, to obtain additional financing or refinancing as may be required and, ultimately, to attain profitable operations. The management of Generice believes that the company will continue to meet its obligations on a timely basis and will achieve profitable operations.

It would be difficult to imagine wording more potentially damaging to future financing than that shown above. How many investors or creditors would find such a qualification easy to accept? Not many! Why would the outside CPA firm insist on such a negative statement? Because they want to protect themselves from future lawsuits. The Big Eight accounting firms in particular, with their large malpractice insurance policies, are big targets for all manner of lawsuits by shareholders, creditors, and other parties.

With a monumental effort, the CPA-audited financial statements were finished by late March. The management and the board of directors were really on the horns of a dilemma. The management team was in place, a hastily prepared "new look" spring catalog was set for printing, and other venture capitalists had been contacted regarding mezzanine financing. In short, critical mass seemed to have been reached. The only thing lacking was that Generice was losing money at an incredibly fast pace. (Such circumstances are not entirely foreign to venture capitalists. New ventures often require the short-term financing of losing operations while establishing market position. That is, after all, one of the primary functions of risk takers.)

The Generice board of directors decided to put the CPA-prepared statements on hold until the results of the spring mailing were determined. It wouldn't take long. Within eight weeks, approximately 98 percent of all mail orders would be received. Other things being equal, if the respondency rate were appreciably higher than previous mailings and the other key measures of performance were improving, it might still be worth trying to finance Generice with new and additional venture capital funding.

Unfortunately, other things were not equal. The results of the spring mailing were only slightly better than the previous efforts—a 1.0 percent pull rate. Exacerbating the problems even further, unbeknownst to all but the most intimately involved officers, directors, and attorneys for the company, it was discovered in early March that the District Attorney's Office of Cuyahoga County was considering a legal action against Generice as well as against Brian Thatcher, individually.

The problem originated in October 1986, when Generice moved to its new facility. In the chaos of the move, hundreds of orders were inadvertently lost, misplaced, or discarded. Seventy-five percent of the cases were simply a matter of missed sales opportunities, because Generice had a policy of not charging customers' credit card accounts until the merchandise was actually picked up by UPS.

In the remaining 25 percent of the cases, Generice's customers sent checks with their orders. Generice's finance department immediately deposited these items into the company's checking account because some checks took as long as two weeks to clear, and management understandably did not want to ship product until funds were determined to be good. However, when the check-paying customers whose orders had been lost did not receive their merchandise within a reasonable time and could get no satisfaction from customer service representatives, they called the D.A.'s office to complain.

After about 20 such instances, the D.A. decided to look into the matter. The deputy district attorney investigating the complaints was not satisfied with the company's (Thatcher's) response that the orders had simply been lost or misplaced. He wanted to get the problem cleaned up quickly, and he admonished Brian Thatcher not to allow a recurrence. Thatcher consented to this. Over the next several months, Generice's attorneys and the deputy D.A. developed the paperwork to formally document an injunction barring Generice from cashing customer checks when products were not available for delivery within 60 days of the receipt of the orders.

The situation took a decided turn for the worse in March when it became apparent that Generice was continuing to accept customer checks while some of the manufacturers whose products had been ordered were refusing to ship merchandise until past-due invoices were paid. Since the company could barely pay its ongoing bills, Generice was unwittingly placed in the position of being unable to perform under the terms of the permanent injunction. Management clearly would not have deliberately ignored the deputy D.A.

An extremely tight cash flow was the root of the problem. By the time the board of directors fully understood the facts, the magnitude of the problem had grown. Almost $150,000 in customer deposits had been accepted for which there was (1) no merchandise in inventory, (2) no cash to purchase the required product, and (3) no way to return the funds. Notwithstanding the fact that customer deposits are legally just unsecured general claims, Brian Thatcher became somewhat obsessed with the idea that he could face possible criminal prosecution for allowing this situation to go unattended. That factor had a lot to do with the final disposition of Generice.

In late May 1987, the board of directors of Generice met to decide the company's fate. The meeting began with a status report on Generice's cash position. The chief financial officer stated that at the present pace, the company would be out of cash by mid-June. In addition, it was noted that the number of lawsuits filed by creditors seeking to collect past-due invoices had jumped from three to seven since the last board meeting. And finally, the landlord had just that morning delivered a pay-or-quit notice informing Generice that it had three days to pay the rent due or face an eviction within two weeks.

Generice clearly would not be able to reorganize its financial affairs unless additional funds were made available. Unfortunately, management had already gone to that well earlier in the year. Although they do have a high tolerance for risk, venture capitalists are not given to making repeated investments in enterprises incapable of being saved. The decision had already been made that no additional money would be infused by existing venture capital investors unless new investors could be found. A faint effort was made, but in reality the business was hopelessly insolvent. The only question that remained was how the business should be closed.

After several hours, the board of directors adopted the following action steps to discontinue operation of Generice. First, a meeting would be held with the deputy D.A. to discuss the extremely fragile financial condition of the company. The likelihood of Generice's filing a voluntary Chapter 7 was now quite high, but management would assure the D.A. that refunds of all customer deposits would be made before the filing took place.

Brian Thatcher, of course, was extremely relieved by this decision. Some of the outside directors were also concerned about the possibility of being named in a suit by the D.A.'s office. Everyone concerned (including legal advisers) was certain the action would be proven without merit, but even the appearance of impropriety could have adverse implications for upstanding financial citizens such as the venture capitalists who had invested in Generice.

Second, a meeting would be arranged with representatives of the largest, and only secured, creditor Generice had—the printer of its catalogs. That vendor had a standard credit policy of requiring all accounts with credit balances in excess of $250,000 to secure the line of credit with a blanket lien on all assets. More than a year prior to Generice's problems, the appropriate documents were executed and filed with the necessary state agency. Generice's outstanding balance to that creditor had grown to over $1.3 million. Management would assure the printing company that it would cooperate fully and Generice would not be filing Chapter 11.

The value of Generice's assets, if they were liquidated by a court-appointed trustee, would not come close to paying off the amount owed to that secured creditor. With the creditor's consent, Generice's management would do everything in its power to dispose of the merchandise and other assets at the highest prices possible, prior to filing the bankruptcy petition. This would include conducting Father's Day and lost-our-lease sales. In consideration for Generice's cooperation, the printing concern would allow the first $125,000 in proceeds to be used to refund customer deposits.

Third, a meeting would be held with all employees to inform them that Generice would be closing its doors at the end of June. Speculation was rife within the company already that Generice was not going to survive. The time had come to put the rumors to rest. Some risk is associated with being so candid with employees. Their daily contacts with customers, suppliers, vendors, and other interested parties make it very difficult to keep the lid on the matter—even when it is in their best interests. Nevertheless, it was decided that employees deserve a chance to find alternatives.

Fourth and last, Brian Thatcher would meet with an attorney specializing in bankruptcy law for the sole purpose of completing all of the appropriate documents necessary for the filing of a voluntary Chapter 7 bankruptcy petition. Thereupon Generice would cease its corporate existence. (Making a general assignment for the benefit of creditors was an option thoroughly explored by the board of directors, but they decided the *finality* of a Chapter 7 was the preferred course of action given the unusual circumstances with the district attorney.

All of the action steps were implemented within 30 days. The final step—the actual filing of the voluntary petition under Chapter 7—was accomplished without fanfare, as the board and management wished. The special insolvency counsel sent a terse notice to "all creditors, their agents and attorneys, and marshals and sheriffs" informing them that Generice had filed bankruptcy. Included in the legal notice were the following:

1. You cannot do *any act* to collect your claim, including telephoning or otherwise communicating with the debtor.
2. You cannot file a lawsuit or continue any existing lawsuit against the debtor.
3. You cannot enforce any judgment against the debtor.
4. You cannot do *any act* to enforce a lien against the debtor's property.
5. You may apply to the court for relief from the restraining order under the provisions set forth in 11 U.S.C., 362.

Within two weeks another notice was sent to all interested parties from a judge of the U.S. Bankruptcy Court. The notice indicated that a meeting of creditors—a 341(a) meeting, in the language of bankruptcy lawyers—would take place in four weeks. The missive also highlighted the following:

> *Special Notice.* It appears from the schedules of the debtor that there are no assets from which any dividend can be paid to creditors. It is unnecessary for any creditor to file his claim at this time

in order to share in any distribution from the estate. If it subsequently appears that there are assets from which a dividend may be paid, creditors will be so notified and given an opportunity to file their claims.

The unsecured general creditors of Generice, who held more than $3.7 million in claims, were stopped in their tracks from trying to get their money. Of course, the shareholders of Generice were also completely wiped out. To a casual observer of the scene, it appears the battleground is strewn only with losing participants. Does anyone come out a winner in this sad state of affairs? Is there actually a recapitalization strategy here? Yes. As noted at the outset of this chapter, creditors expect debtors to fight to the very end. Taking the course that Generice did enabled management to retain the initiative.

With the relatively few exceptions that resulted in independent legal actions, the vast majority of creditors were never given the opportunity to develop strong feelings of hostility toward Generice management. Had the company decided to fight with creditors in a Chapter 11 case, a great deal of enmity would probably have developed. As it turned out, Generice's owners, managers, employees, and creditors were able to quickly move on to other pursuits. Recapitalizing Generice meant a rapid freeing of *human capital* to search for other business and personal opportunities rather than waste additional resources.

CONCLUSION

As I have tried to demonstrate in the preceding chapters of this book, the complex problems related to excessive amounts of debt are nonsexist and nondiscriminatory. Women have proven themselves to be just as able as men to lead their companies down the road to financial trouble. All types of businesses in every industry and geographic region of the country are subject to the ravages of debt-driven financial troubles. I have also attempted to show that businesses can be adversely impacted during periods of economic expansion as well as during recessions. Naturally, the difficulties are more severe during periods of economic contraction. And since the likelihood of the latter event is very strong, highly leveraged business owners, managers, and their advisers should be preparing themselves for another round of survival.

Every financially troubled business forced by its secured or unsecured creditors to the edge of the abyss has a unique solution to its problems. The task, obviously, is to solve the puzzle leading to the recapitalization of the enterprise rather than to its demise. There is clearly a place in business revitalization programs for court-administered solutions. In fact, in the absence of settlements negotiated out of court, it is highly probable that unresolved financial disputes will be referred to the bankruptcy court for disposition. However, far more avenues available outside the courtroom are more effective, less rigid, and less costly. I wish you good luck in finding your solution.

INDEX